GREAT ENTREPRENEURS

GREAT ENTREPRENEURS

ARE FOUND ON THE OTHER SIDE OF
THE PRESSURE

Stories of Overcoming, Belief, and Unstoppable Ambition

KEMONE S-G BROWN-TSHABALALA

TAMARiND HiLL
.PRESS

Published by Tamarind Hill Press in 2023

Copyright © Kemone S-G Brown-Tshabalala 2023

Kemone S-G Brown-Tshabalala has asserted her right under the Copyright, Designs and Patents Act of 1988 to be identified as the author of this work.

This book is a work of non-fiction based on the lives, experiences, and recollections of the contributors featured. In some limited cases, names of people, places, dates, sequences, or the detail of events have been changed [solely] to protect the privacy of others. The author has stated to the publishers that, except in such minor respects not affecting the substantial accuracy of the work, the contents of this book are true.

This book is sold, subject to the condition that it shall not, by way of trade or otherwise, be lent, resold, hired out, or otherwise circulated without the publisher's prior consent in any form of binding or cover other than that in which it is published and without a similar condition, including this condition being imposed on the subsequent purchaser.

All rights reserved. No part of this publication may be reproduced, stored in a retrievable system, or transmitted in any form or by any means, electronic, mechanical photocopying, recording or otherwise, without the permission of the author and copyright owner.

First published in Great Brittain by

Tamarind Hill Press

G33 Evans Incubation Centre, Durham Way South, Newton Aycliffe Business Park, County Durham, DL5 6XP

www.tamarindhillpress.com

Tamarind Hill Press Limited Reg. No. 14023099

A CIP catalogue record for this book is available from the British Library.

PRINT ISBN: 978-1-915161-72-7

eBook ISBN: 978-1-915161-76-5

TAMARiND HiLL
.PRESS

Dedication

For my daughter, Oratile Tshukudu, and the other young aspiring female entrepreneurs, who are looking up to all of us in this book. May you all grow into women who refuse to give up on your dreams of becoming successful Black women in business.

TABLE OF CONTENTS

Dedication V
Foreword VIII
Preface X
Acknowledgements XIII
Introduction 15
Shawnafi Dynesen Anderson 19
   Your Rights are Non-negotiable 19
   Who is she? 32
Kamila Aletha Atherley 38
   Nurturing Hearts and Families Through Innovative Care 38
   Who is she? 44
Christina Brooks 48
   Lead with Conviction 48
   Who is she? 58
Kemone S-G Brown-Tshabalala 62
   Every Problem has a Solution; Find it 62
   Who is she? 79
Yushima Cherry-Burks 83
   Empowering Survivor Healing and Advocacy 83
   Who is she? 89
Alecia Latoya Henry 94
   Beauty in Entrepreneurship and Creativity 94
   Who is she? 101
Janair Johnson 106
   Resilience in Every Step 106
   Who is she? 114

Dudu Mathebula 119
Be Ready to Adapt to Change 119
Who is she? 124
Loreen Aisha Ochefu-Ogiri 128
Just Move 128
Who is she? 137
Omotinuola Oladeji 140
A Visionary Entrepreneur and Inspiring Philanthropist 140
Who is she? 150
Mrs Omitade Omoshalewa 155
Equitable and Inclusive Business 155
Who is she? 160
Nikki Porcher 164
Quitting has Never Crossed My Mind 164
Who is she? 170
Patrice Reid 174
Transforming the World of Skincare 174
Who is she? 177
Dikeledi Ndoni Sibanda 182
When Passion and Creativity Meets Entrepreneurship 182
Who is she? 188
Veneish Tanneisha Wallace 192
Quality Caregiving is Underpinned by the Innate Human Spirit 192
Who is she? 201
Closing Remarks 207

Foreword

One word that comes to mind when thinking of my very dear friend, Kemone Brown-Tshabalala, is altruism. Being the selfless activist who always wants to help others, to give the voiceless a voice, to care and fight for the love of the cause, to give people the opportunity to discover themselves, she made it possible for these women across the world to share their stories by having created this platform.

The stories shared in *Great Entrepreneurs ... Are Found on the Other Side of the Pressure* can be everyone's story. For some readers, it may be because they have gone through the same experiences, while for others, it may be experiences waiting to happen. The many faces of abuse, ensuing suffering, trauma, deceit, and hurt encountered by these women are relatable and may perhaps open up old wounds, or it may just be the long awaited remedy or ointment to help with the restoration process. These brave women, who despite their experiences, trauma, challenges, hardships, dips, and slips, picked themselves up and got it made against all odds.

No one has a clear view of the world or can do much while laying down, and the authors have demonstrated it so well through their stories. When life knocked them down in one way or the other, they bounced back, got up, and started afresh. Take aways from their stories are that staying down in the mud, accepting defeat and being complacent, should not and must never be an option. Complacency is the thief of opportunities, development, progress, and success. A woman and a Black woman more so, maybe because of our circumstances, can make a plan like nobody else. We find ways and means to get out of the mess, ways to make it happen, not only for ourselves but also for all near and dear to us. Entrepreneurship and/or ingenuity are often borne out of these plans and this is the beauty on the other side of life's pressures.

One commonality throughout these compelling stories is that becoming an entrepreneur requires tenacity; it tests one's mettle to survive in the world of industry, business, academia, or wherever life takes you. The Kemones, the Dikeledis, the Alecias may be from different walks of life, from diverse backgrounds across the globe, but these women have learnt to confront challenges, to fight atrocious systems and to believe in themselves.

Readers, get ready to make that mind shift, believe in yourself, go over into action, eliminate obstacles, take risks, acknowledge limitations, pull out all stops, and make your dream come true. Your entrepreneurial ventures may just rub off on a young girl from a place far afield.

Thank you Kemone, thank you brave sisters, for having shaken us out of our state of ignorance, out of our state of oblivion, for having created an awareness of the stark realities out there, for having ignited a spark in us to effect change, and for having given us the tools to master the art of living and surviving in a world filled with uncertainties, negativity and atrocities. God bless your beautiful souls.

Onward and upward.

Ella
Elvira Lottering

Preface

I've never imagined my life without running a business; it's just always been something I knew I wanted to do. Regardless of the different career paths I've explored, the drive to create something of my own has remained constant. Whether it's been a side hustle or a full-fledged business, I've known that taking charge of my financial destiny was essential.

Over the years, I've had the privilege of establishing my own businesses, juggling multiple side ventures, and assisting numerous entrepreneurs in their startup journeys. Through this experience, I've witnessed the resilience of businesses that withstand the test of time and the necessary closures that sometimes occur. Some entrepreneurs pivot because they must, while others regrettably abandon their dreams. I've both built and helped others build successful businesses.

In my capacity as a mentor and coach, I've had a front-row seat to entrepreneurs grappling with the unique challenges of their businesses. More often than not, I've played a pivotal role in guiding them through these challenges, enabling them to emerge with valuable lessons, innovative strategies, and the launch or revitalization of their businesses, often resulting in newfound profitability or, for some, the realization of profits for the first time.

One of the most rewarding things about being good at what you do is that the people you help will refer other people to you. Indeed, word-of-mouth marketing is alive and kicking. After years of working as a business coach and mentor, facing the challenge of not being able to accommodate as many clients as I wished, I made the decision to initiate business workshops and retreats catering to entrepreneurs at various stages of their journey. Hosting these retreats introduced me to fresh perspectives and confronted me with unprecedented challenges. It compelled me to explore innovative solutions to assist entrepreneurs in overcoming these obstacles, fostering my own growth and development as a mentor and coach. This book is a product of one such transformative retreat experience.

Early last year, I organized a virtual retreat for women who, like me, are entrepreneurs and businesswomen. This retreat was centred around healing and provided support for women who had encountered or were still grappling with trauma in their personal lives and business journeys. I conceived this event because I've faced numerous challenges that were meant to undermine both me and my businesses. However, through a range of strategies, I've consistently managed to overcome these obstacles and persevere on my entrepreneurial path, and now share them with other entrepreneurs.

Many of the women who attended the retreat shared that it was an uplifting and empowering experience, and I wholeheartedly concur. Witnessing women with backgrounds akin to mine triumph over their traumas and continue to operate ethical, prosperous businesses was truly inspirational. What struck me profoundly were the narratives of Black women in particular. Although we share many similarities with others, our experiences diverge in numerous ways due to various factors. Often, Black women lack access to vital resources, including education, emotional support, financial backing, psychological assistance, physical resources, and more, which are readily available to other racial groups. Nevertheless, we persist, surmounting barriers and achieving success in our entrepreneurial ventures.

Unfortunately, many Black women find themselves facing a different set of challenges. In addition to the aforementioned hurdles, they often lack the necessary resilience and willpower to surmount the obstacles blocking their path to entrepreneurial success. This shortfall is frequently a result of not realizing their full potential, even in the face of limited resources and the weight of their personal trials and tribulations.

Recognizing this disparity, I conceived this initiative aimed at promoting and inspiring Black women in business and entrepreneurship. As an author and researcher, I believe that the written word can serve as a powerful medium for advancing this cause. I decided to write a book, and extended invitation to Black female entrepreneurs around the world to join me in telling their stories to encourage Black females into entrepreneurship and business. I am grateful to those who accepted the invitation and shared their stories.

The motivation behind this book also stems from the recognition that, despite the numerous retreats and the potential influx of new clients, it's nearly impossible to reach everyone individually. Each day, I am forced to decline requests for one-on-one mentorship due to the limitations of time. There are only so many hours available for such personalized guidance, as well as constraints on the number of retreats, workshops, webinars, courses, and trainings I can develop within a year. This reality often leaves individuals in need without timely access to the assistance they seek, especially from their desired source.

Even though I acknowledge that there will still be people beyond my reach with the publication of this book, it represents a means to extend my reach to a broader audience. I hope it will have an even greater impact.

As you read these pages, I encourage you to absorb the wisdom, courage, and insights shared by these remarkable women. Their journeys are a testament to the incredible strength that resides within each of us, waiting to be awakened and harnessed. It is my deepest aspiration that their stories will inspire you, empower you, and propel you forward on your own entrepreneurial path.

To your success,

Kemone S-G Brown-Tshabalala

Acknowledgements

While this book may not be religious in nature, its existence is a testament to the divine intervention and guidance that have seen me through moments of doubt and adversity. To God, I owe You my gratitude for the strength to persist. You are the source of all blessings and the guiding light of my life; I offer my deepest gratitude. Your presence and divine grace have carried me through every aspect of my life. You have blessed me beyond measure, and for that, I am eternally thankful.

To the best wife in the world, Kelebogile Tshabalala, your support and belief in my abilities make me feel unstoppable. God for sure knew what He was doing when He made you, and I am forever grateful we were chosen for each other. Thank you for the sacrifices you make to ensure that I chase my dreams relentlessly. I cannot express how grateful I am for your presence in my life.

To my dad, George Washington Brown, for your unconditional love and support, I am the luckiest girl alive. God gave me the greatest gift when he made you my dad. Thank you for supporting everything I do, no matter how big or small, and for making me feel as though I am the best at anything and everything. Thank you for always being there for me. Life would be impossible without you. I love you, Daddy!

To Ella, you have been there for me in so many ways over the years and continue to support my dreams. Thank you so much for taking the time to read this book and give me your feedback. I appreciate you more than you know.

To the remarkable women who entrusted me with their stories, the inspiring individuals I've had the privilege to collaborate with over the years, and all those who have played a role in bringing this book to fruition, I extend my heartfelt thanks. Your contributions and support have breathed life into these pages, and I am profoundly appreciative of each of you.

Finally, to those who have embraced this book by purchasing or reading it, your interest and engagement fill me with immense gratitude. I am humbled by your support, and it is with deep appreciation that I offer my thanks.

Introduction

In the heart of every entrepreneur lies a profound narrative — a story of ambition, resilience, and the pursuit of success. Within these pages, you are about to embark on a journey into the lives of exceptional Black women entrepreneurs who are navigating the turbulent waters of business with determination.

As part of this collection, I have included a reflection of my own entrepreneurial journey and some of the challenges I have faced and the lesson learned. My goal is to empower Black female entrepreneurs by showcasing the experiences of successful women who, despite their achievements, continue to encounter challenges, both in their personal and professional lives. It was important to me that this book not solely reflect my own perspective. I firmly believe that featuring diverse narratives of Black women from various backgrounds, from different countries and engaged in a wide range of businesses, will provide aspiring entrepreneurs, those facing difficulties in their entrepreneurial journey, and even those who have achieved success, with relatable stories. It offers them the chance to connect with at least one woman in the book who mirrors their own experiences in one way or another.

They are remarkable women who defy odds, surmounting adversities daily. They transcend the role of mere entrepreneurs, transforming into inspiration and hope for others navigating their own trials. The narratives you hold within these pages bear witness to the challenges that these women have had to overcome, serving as a tribute to the enduring spirit that resides within Black women entrepreneurs. Within these pages lies a treasury of stories resonating with the cadence of perseverance, innovation, and empowerment. These narratives are the heartbeats of Black women who have confronted adversity head-on and chosen to emerge triumphant against all odds.

As you turn these pages, you'll encounter tales that transcend the conventional boundaries of business literature. Here, you'll delve into the personal stories of these remarkable women, of battles fought not only in business but also in the recesses of their own minds. These are stories of dreams that refused to be silenced, of businesses birthed from the crucible of challenge.

Each narrative unveils a moment of truth, a pivotal juncture where the path of entrepreneurship met head-on with life's harshest tests. These are not stories of easy triumphs, but of struggles that tested courage and resolve. These women have shared their vulnerabilities, their moments of doubt, and the hurdles that might have discouraged lesser souls. However, they also share how they harnessed their pain to fuel their determination, how they turned setbacks into comebacks, and how they transformed challenges into opportunities.

As you immerse yourself in these stories, you will notice a common thread woven through each narrative; the undeniable belief in possibility. These women did not allow their circumstances to define their destinies. Instead, they carved their paths, pioneering businesses that resonate with purpose and authenticity. Their journeys remind us that entrepreneurship isn't just about financial gain; it's about carving a space where dreams can flourish, where innovation can thrive, and where the power to effect change can be harnessed.

Thus, this book isn't just a collection of stories; it's a movement, a call to action, a clarion call for empowerment. These pages are an invitation, extended not just to the women who have shared their stories, but to every Black woman who dreams of stepping into the world of entrepreneurship. It's a testament to the fact that, despite the obstacles that may arise from systemic inequalities, resource disparities, and the weight of history, the spirit of entrepreneurship knows no colour, no gender, and no boundary.

Here, you will find narratives that lift you up, ignite your aspirations, and spark the fire of resilience within you. These stories are a rallying cry, inviting you to join a community of dreamers, doers, and changemakers. Through these women's experiences, you'll learn that challenges are not roadblocks, but stepping stones, opportunities to discover your true strength and your limitless potential.

The stories you're about to read are a tribute to the power of storytelling, the power of shared experiences, and the power of unity. We're not just reading tales; we're participating in a collective journey, amplifying voices that have often been marginalized, and celebrating the achievements that have been overshadowed for far too long.

To every reader, every dreamer, every entrepreneur, prepare to be inspired. The courage, the tenacity, and the sheer audacity of these women will resonate with you long after you've closed this book. As you embark on this literary journey, remember that the stories contained within these pages are just the beginning. The real journey, the real empowerment, begins when you find the echoes of your own story within these narratives, and you recognize that your journey, too, is worth sharing, celebrating, and championing.

Embrace the stories, embrace the lessons, and embrace the boundless potential that lies within you. Your dreams are waiting. It's time to turn the page and step into your own story of resilience beyond boundaries.

To ensure that you get the most from this process, I have also created a workbook, with exercises carefully designed to empower you as an entrepreneur. Search, **Great Entrepreneur in Training**. These exercises will help you unlock your potential and help you stay committed to your entrepreneurial journey.

"My mission in life is not merely to survive, but to thrive; and to do so with some passion, some compassion, some humor, and some style."
- **Maya Angelou**

Shawnafi Dynesen Anderson

Your Rights are Non-negotiable

"Even in the face of overwhelming odds, standing your ground and seeking legal assistance is a form of self-liberation. It's a declaration that you refuse to be controlled, that you have the agency to shape your destiny, and that your rights are non-negotiable."

The first thing that I want you to understand is that life itself can be full of challenges. Trials and tribulations can come in any form, not just in your business life or in your pursuit of entrepreneurship, but every single aspect of your life. Regardless of what challenges you face, no matter what you have been through, you can survive it; you can thrive and become successful in the things you set out to do.

My own challenges started from as young as 10 years old, and even in adulthood, I've had quite a few life challenges. I have survived child abuse, which included sexual abuse by someone who claimed to be my father — a decorated educator in Jamaica — for three years. Even as a child, I knew that what was happening was wrong and I tried everything to get out of that situation. I turned to many adults in the family, seeking help, but was often told that I was not his daughter anyway, so it was okay for them to turn a blind eye.

I suffered so much but the most hurtful thing was that no adult saw the need to help. No one saw the need to answer my cries of wanting to be taken out of that home. When I went from being a straight A student to an F student in less than three months after I started living with my so-called father, no one noticed or tried to figure out what was wrong. I still have scars from being beaten because I spoke up about my sexual abuse; that's how much no one cared.

After suffering for three years, one day, I was beaten so bad and locked in a room at my father's house. A relative came to visit and was adamant that I be taken to the doctor because of the condition that I was in. My so-called father reluctantly took me to the doctor, but lied about what had happened to me. Instead of telling them that he'd beaten me so bad after I refused to let him sexually assault me for the millionth time, he told them that he lost his temper because he caught me with a boy. I was only thirteen. I had no interest in boys because I hated to think that I would have to go through what my father was putting me through at the hands of anyone else.

The doctors took a lot of evidence of my bruises and sent it to the police, but nothing came out of it. I was made to go back home with my abuser and, unfortunately, the abuse did not end. On my thirteenth birthday, that fell on a Thursday, he bought me a birthday cake. No other adult was in the home. I was home with my father and stepsister. However, he sent my stepsister across town to buy something. She was only nine at the time, so it was obvious that he wanted her out of the house to do whatever he wanted with me as usual.

I remember him telling me that I had to perform sexual favours if I wanted the cake. I kept refusing, and he beat me to a pulp. I was so angry that I told him that I'd take his life and burn the house down. It was a terrible thing to say but I'd had enough. For three years, I had suffered at the hand of this man who was supposed to be my father and here he was ruining the one day in the year when I was supposed to be experiencing joy. It was enough. I couldn't take it anymore. It was this outcry that inadvertently became my salvation because it was then that he shipped me off to reform school.

As you can imagine, this experience taught me the art of survival from an age when most children remain unburdened by such harsh realities. I had to learn to keep going, regardless of my trauma and pain — that my pain wasn't the sum of my identity. The resilience that took root within me at such a young age became the cornerstone of who I am. It became the guiding force that would shape my future pursuits, both personal and professional. In the shadows of my past, I found not just pain, but a source of strength that continues to fuel my journey. Thus, my ability to navigate the turbulent waters of life was not born in the calm, but in the storm of my early experiences.

My childhood trauma did not end there. Yet, amidst the many upheavals, I realized that my future laid in my hands alone. The halls of education provided me with both an escape and a source of empowerment, a lifeline to a world free from the chains of my past. I knew that by doing well in school, I could pursue a life in a place where no one knew of my trauma and I could have a fresh start. I completed my high school education and then went to college. None of it was easy. There was so much that I went through during the time but I succeeded regardless.

God always sent strangers to help me and many of them left a mark on my life. It was through meeting a stranger that I was able to finish college as he helped me financially. Someone who would offer much more. He was one of the very first people outside of my family who I confided in about what I had gone through and was going through at the time. The act of confiding in a stranger felt liberating — a cathartic release that liberated my voice from its self-imposed prison. Each word spoken was a shard of my soul, offered to the universe, and met with an understanding ear. This stranger became the conduit through which my story was acknowledged and validated. It was as if, in that moment, he bore witness to the invisible scars etched on my being.

The empathy he exhibited during our conversation became a balm for my wounded heart. It was a reminder that, even in a world marred by pain, there were those who were willing to listen, to hold space, and to offer solace. His presence was an embodiment of the simple yet profound truth — our stories have the power to heal, both the teller and the listener.

This encounter marked a transformation within me. It was a shift from viewing vulnerability as a weakness to understanding it as a wellspring of strength. The walls I had erected around my heart began to crumble, allowing empathy to seep in. It was through this vulnerability that I realized I was not alone in my struggles.

Later, in adulthood, my path became one of many twists and turns, spanning across continents and cultures, bringing together experiences that would shape my understanding of stability, love, and the pursuit of self-discovery. The first time I left Jamaica, I journeyed to Germany with the man I was in a relationship with. Germany greeted me with opulence and excess — a lifestyle that left me longing for the simplicity of my roots. The chasm between wealth and comfort became evident, and in the presence of affluence, I discovered the invaluable worth of authenticity and contentment. I wasn't the right match for the person I was with, so I soon returned home to Jamaica to see what life had to offer. I can still remember my mother calling me a fool for walking away from the riches I was offered. Although her remarks were hurtful, I knew that I did not have it in me to face even half the pain I had faced in adulthood as I had done in childhood. I refused to stay in a relationship without love, no matter the amount of money the man had.

Back in Jamaica and needing to decide what I was going to do with my life, I enrolled in an IT course. It was through this that I met my first husband, who was from Sweden. I created a dating site as my class project and he signed on to it. He asked me to move with him to Sweden and I visited him for a trial run. Transitions came with their fair share of challenges. We experience language barriers and there were cultural nuances. Moreover, I did not like his living accommodation. I lived in a house in Jamaica, while he lived in an apartment. The only apartment I knew back then in the 90s were those in the ghettoes of Kingston and there was no way I was moving overseas to live like that. Of course, that was simply a lack of cultural understanding as it was a beautiful apartment; I didn't understand this back then.

We agreed that I would travel back to Jamaica and he would get a house and other things in place then I would move back to Sweden. He did that and I moved to Sweden to live with him fulltime. We got married. Returning to Sweden, I bore a dual purpose — to fortify my educational foundation and forge a life that aligned with my convictions. Given our relationship up to then, my dreams included him in them. However, the duality of my desires mirrored the complexity of life itself, and the contrast between the high-rise apartment and my yearning for authenticity was a reminder that stability isn't always synonymous with fulfilment.

As we navigated our relationship, I struggled with notions of love, vulnerability, and partnership, discovering that relationships should nurture growth, not suppress individuality. While my journey involved companionship, it also highlighted the importance of choosing paths that resonate with one's own aspirations, rather than compromising for the sake of others. Through every step, my determination to carve my own path grew stronger. The pursuit of education expanded my horizons, opening doors to opportunities I had never fathomed. Yet, it wasn't without its emotional trials. The friction with my mother, her perception of my choices, and my conviction to prove my worth all added layers to my narrative.

Things were not working out between me and my then husband and we decided to separate. Then, in 2012, there was a turning point, marked by unexpected news; I was pregnant. Despite the rift in our relationship, circumstances kept us sharing the same house, a situation fraught with tension and unspoken words. Our home, once a refuge, became a battleground of underlying emotions and suppressed turmoil.

Compelled by the awareness that my foster children's future hung in the balance, I navigated the challenging terrain, straddling the line between estranged partners and cohabitants. Our worlds collided in a paradoxical dance as we raised the children under the same roof. In 2015, weary of this stasis, I yearned for change. I set my sights on a remote village, a place that resonated with my memories of St. Thomas, Jamaica. Determined to carve my space, I purchased a house, an act that symbolized my reclamation of autonomy.

In the heart of this transformation, fate cast a new figure onto the stage of my life — my current husband. With him came the promise of companionship and a chance to explore new territories of love. But as fate would have it, the complexities multiplied when I realized that my ex-husband had moved into the house with me, rewriting the boundaries of my narrative once again.

I could not continue to live in a house with my ex and decided to travel to Jamaica to get away from him and his antics. With my new partner in Jamaica, caring for both our youngest child and my ailing mother, I returned to Sweden in 2018. It was a chance to rebuild, to confront my ex-husband's persistent presence, and to find some semblance of peace. I wanted him to move out of the house that I had bought with my own money and leave me to live in peace.

However, as fate would have it, my ex-husband's actions swiftly thrust me into a storm. I wanted to establish boundaries, and he retaliated by refusing to vacate the house, asserting his rights as a co-owner in a legal system that recognized no middle ground between marriage and divorce.

In his attempt to assert control, he began showing signs of stalking and manipulation, behaviours that echoed the haunting patterns of my past. This unmasking of the darker aspects of his character was a painful revelation — one that compelled me to scrutinize my choices and prioritize my well-being. My ex-husband refused to cooperate. Due to his escalating actions, I made the painful choice to relinquish the house, severing the ties that bound me to a place that had once been home. The path forward was strewn with heartache, yet the act of reclaiming my autonomy marked a victory. It was an assertion that my present and future were mine to shape.

The difficulties of my past rippled into my present, leaving me at a crossroads. I knew I had to look after myself first and foremost, and so, my marriage with my ex-husband, which only existed due to co-parenting and shared responsibilities by then, culminated in a divorce in 2019. It was an arduous decision, one filled with heartache, introspection, and the realization that my pursuit of happiness was not incompatible with my duty to my children. The marriage I embarked on with my current husband mirrored the resilience I had cultivated within myself. It became a testament to the understanding that love, while boundless, must also be mindful of each individual's growth.

The years following my divorce were a saga of unrelenting challenges, where the shadows of control and manipulation cast their long reach into my life once again. It was a phase marked by a twisted dance of reports, accusations, and interference masterminded by my ex-husband — a continued effort to assert dominance and undermine my well-being. I was going to have to fight for myself and my children.

Having once navigated treacherous waters, I was equipped with the knowledge that survival required more than mere endurance; it required strategic adaptation. With my children's well-being at the forefront of my mind, I employed a multi-pronged approach to counteract his tactics.

Understanding the bureaucratic systems that he attempted to weaponize, I pre-emptively made my business appear to be in financial turmoil, a calculated move that curbed his attempts to gain control over it. I also fortified my legal defences, seeking the counsel of professionals well-versed in the complexities of family law. This strategic manoeuvring allowed me to shield my business and assets, thwarting his relentless quest for dominance.

Amid this harrowing battle, the support of friends and allies was my lifeline. My extensive experience as a foster parent and therapist had instilled in me a vast network of connections, a community that rallied around me during my darkest moments. Armed with their support and my will to protect my children, I confronted each fabricated report and baseless accusation.

However, my decision was also tempered by the realization that the familiar confines of Sweden offered no respite from my husband's relentless onslaught. It was against this backdrop that the prospect of a fresh start beckoned — a chance to sever the last vestiges of his control and craft a new narrative for myself and my children. So, the decision to move to the UK emerged. This was a chance to escape the stranglehold that had bound me for so long.

In this new chapter, the embrace of a different culture and the opportunity to explore a fresh landscape infused me with a renewed sense of purpose. The complexities of my past, the battles I fought, and the strength that carried me through it all converged into a narrative of transformation. With each stride forward, I was shedding the remnants of manipulation and control, replacing them with a newfound sense of empowerment.

This new chapter was marked by both the pursuit of my own dreams and the nurturing of my children's aspirations. The move to the UK offered a canvas on which I could paint the picture of my desires, with the knowledge that I had earned the right to shape my destiny. The relentless pursuit of control by my ex-husband was now but a whisper in the wind.

Unfortunately, stepping onto UK soil, hoping for a new beginning, I found myself embroiled in a new wave of challenges that seemed to eclipse even the troubled past I had left behind. The shadow of control and manipulation had followed me across borders, manifesting as threats, legal battles, and attempts to force my return to the life I had fought so hard to escape. This period tested my resilience and will power like never before.

Armed with a lawyer, I fortified my defences and confronted each new threat with the knowledge that I was no longer alone in this battle. The importance of standing my ground became evident in the firestorm of legal manoeuvres that sought to disempower me. The petition to have my children taken from me was a calculated move designed to yank me back into a web of control. I refused to bow. I understood that capitulating would mean a return to the chains I had fought so hard to break. Instead, I confronted the challenge head-on, channelling my strength and defiance into the battle.

In this process, my children's well-being was my guiding star. Their futures, dreams, and safety were non-negotiable. I took each step with the knowledge that their lives hung in the balance, and I would not allow history to repeat itself. As I stood up against the attempts to force my return, I was also challenging the cycle of control and manipulation that had marked my past.

The chaotic legal battles were a testing ground for my tenacity. Each court hearing, each legal manoeuvre, became an opportunity to demonstrate that my voice mattered, that my autonomy was worth fighting for. My lawyer was my advocate, my partner in this battle against oppression. Together, we dismantled the web of lies woven by my ex-husband and exposed the truth.

One of the lessons I learned on this journey was that even in the face of overwhelming odds and so-called evidence, standing your ground and seeking legal assistance is a form of self-liberation. It's a declaration that you refuse to be controlled, that you have the agency to shape your destiny, and that your rights are non-negotiable. This stance is not just for your personal life; it's for all aspects of it, including in business. Navigating the legal systems in both Sweden and the UK was a test of my patience and strategic thinking. Each country had its own rules, nuances, and hurdles. At times, it felt like I was playing a complex game where the stakes were the well-being of my children and my freedom, thus, having legal representation was a lifeline.

Navigating these challenges also highlighted the importance of community and support. Friends, allies, and professionals who stood by my side became pillars of strength.

In the pursuit of autonomy, justice, and freedom, I learned that standing your ground is not just an act; it's a legacy of resilience and a pledge to craft a future on your own terms. Emotionally, the toll was heavy. The fear of losing my children, the anxiety of false accusations, and the relentless pressure took a toll on my mental and physical well-being. Yet, every day, I looked into my children's eyes and found the courage to keep fighting. The courtroom battles weren't just about legalities; they were also a battleground of emotions. I had to remain composed and focused while facing false narratives about my character and my capabilities as a mother. It was a painful realisation that control and manipulation can extend beyond the confines of personal relationships and seep into the justice system itself. I held onto my belief in justice. The pursuit of truth and fairness drove my determination. I refused to let my ex-husband's lies define me, and I found strength in sharing my story openly, stripping away the shroud of secrecy that often cloaks these battles.

I have shared a very personal story, but this can be extended to your business. As an entrepreneur, you are not separate and apart from your personal life. What you go through in your personal life can significantly impact your business; it affected mine.

For those facing similar battles against control and manipulation, I offer this advice:

1. **Seek Legal Representation:** A qualified lawyer who understands the relevant laws is invaluable.

2. **Build a Support Network:** Surround yourself with friends, family, and professionals who believe in your strength and your cause.

3. **Share Your Story:** Breaking the silence is a powerful act. Sharing your story not only sheds light on the issue but also reinforces the effectiveness of determination.

4. **Prioritize Self-Care:** Taking care of your emotional and mental well-being is crucial. Find healthy ways to cope with stress, such as exercise, therapy, meditation, or engaging in hobbies.

5. **Believe in Yourself:** Remember your worth and your capabilities. Your past does not define your future, and you have the strength to overcome even the most challenging circumstances.

6. **Stay Informed:** Familiarize yourself with your rights and the legal processes in your jurisdiction. Knowledge is empowering and can help you make informed decisions.

7. **Hold onto Hope:** Even in the darkest moments, hold onto the hope that justice will prevail, because it will.

Going through all the turmoil with my ex-husband significantly impacted my business negatively. I became a boss that people did not get along with and some of my staff quit. This meant that I lost valuable customers. As for the women who left, it was difficult as I had built up the business and had nurtured the women who I worked with; I cared for them, so losing them was painful. However, going through this also taught me a lot and made me appreciate how I had worked up to then.

The inception of my business was built upon my personal experience and the desire to offer products that catered specifically to the needs of women of colour. As someone who had personally faced challenges with hair loss, skin issues, and a lack of representation in the beauty industry, I saw an opportunity to not only create effective products but also build a movement that empowered women.

The journey began with a simple idea: to provide natural, effective solutions for common beauty concerns that often went unaddressed by mainstream brands. I started by experimenting with homemade remedies, like the onion oil that kick-started my journey. The turning point came when I decided to step in front of the camera, sharing my experiences and demonstrating the products in live videos. This authenticity and vulnerability resonated with my audience and helped forge a strong connection. It helped me to gain most of them back when the dust settled and I was again able to focus on my business.

The key strategies that have contributed to my business's success and being able to retain customers all over the world include:

1. **Cultural Empathy:** Understanding the unique beauty needs and cultural nuances of the Black community was essential. By tailoring my products to these specific needs, I positioned myself as a brand that genuinely understood and cared about their concerns.

2. **Transparency and Authenticity:** I made authenticity a core value of my brand. Sharing my personal journey, struggles, and triumphs in live videos created a sense of trust and relatability. People could see that I wasn't just selling products; I was genuinely invested in their well-being.

3. **Educational Content:** I leveraged social media to educate my audience about common beauty challenges, ingredients to look for, and how to properly care for their skin and hair. This approach not only established me as an expert but also empowered my customers with knowledge.

4. **Community Building:** I cultivated a community of like-minded individuals who shared their own experiences, tips, and successes.

This sense of belonging and shared purpose fostered strong brand loyalty and advocacy.

5. **Representation Matters:** Representation was a driving force. I featured women of colour in my marketing campaigns, showcasing the beauty and diversity that mainstream media often overlooked. This resonated deeply with my audience and challenged industry norms.

6. **Quality and Innovation:** My products prioritized quality and innovation, addressing the gaps in the market with effective solutions. The results spoke for themselves, which helped dispel scepticism and build credibility.

7. **Testimonials and Social Proof:** The positive experiences and transformations shared by my customers through testimonials and before-and-after photos served as powerful social proof. This played a significant role in building trust and convincing sceptics.

8. **Accessibility and Inclusivity:** I focused on affordability without compromising quality, making my products accessible to a broader range of individuals. This inclusivity was a cornerstone of my mission to empower women from all walks of life.

9. **Consistency and Adaptability:** Consistently delivering on promises and adapting to customer feedback were critical. I iterated on products based on customer input, ensuring their needs were genuinely met.

10. **Sustainability and Ethics:** Demonstrating a commitment to sustainability and ethical practices was important. People want to support brands that align with their values.

What I want you to take away from this is the idea that you must do everything with authenticity in your business. Do not take shortcuts. If you show your customers and staff that you care, they will always support your business. One of the greatest things that happened was how the women who worked with me rallied around me after my legal battles. I had spent almost every bit of income on fighting my ex-husband. My savings had almost depleted and I barely had money to get the business up and running again. When I approached the women to let them know about this, so many of them agreed to loan me the money to keep the business going. It showed me that they believed in what I was doing; there's no better feeling. Together, we were able to rebuild and continue our journey.

Who is she?

Shawnafi Dynesen Anderson is a gifted individual who has not only embraced her life's path but has also transformed lives in so many countries. Bath, St. Thomas being her hometown, Shawnafi is leaving an indelible mark on the world as a holistic healer, skincare formulator, and social entrepreneur.

Unveiling ancestral wisdom, Shawnafi's journey has transcended old-time knowledge into a health and wellness business that helps solve many health problems for her customers. Her prowess as a queen herbalist and holistic medicine artisan is evident through her products that address a plethora of everyday ailments. From hyperpigmentation to menopause symptoms, insomnia to balding, her creations stand as nature's gifts, offering remedies to complex problems. While she humbly avoids calling them medicines, these solutions reflect her deep connection to the healing properties of the earth.

Driven by her own experiences and a deep-seated passion for change, Shawnafi's vision extends beyond individual wellness. A true visionary and wayfarer, she is steadfast in her pursuit of establishing a global wellness and skincare franchise. As the owner of Zyzven Naturals and co-founder of NAFI (Nature's Answer For It), she demonstrates her commitment to empowering women and girls on a grand scale.

Zyzven Naturals, under Shawnafi's guidance, stands as a testament to effective and natural skincare. With a focus on high-performance natural ingredients, her creations target specific skin concerns without resorting to fillers, artificial colours, fragrances, or bleaching agents. Her dedication to authenticity shines through, with 95% of Zyzven Naturals products being vegan. The range caters to diverse skin types, offering respite from conditions like acne, dryness, oily skin, alopecia, and eczema.

As a social entrepreneur, Shawnafi champions sustainable businesses and income generation, aiding both women and men in realizing their potential. Her impact extends beyond her own successes, a testament to her ethos of uplifting others. Proudly representing her roots as a Maroon, Shawnafi uses her voice to create a world where empowerment and well-being flourish.

"In the pursuit of autonomy, justice, and freedom, I learned that standing your ground is not just an act; it's a legacy of resilience and a pledge to craft a future on your own terms."
- **Shawnafi Dynesen Anderson**

Zyzven Naturals
GLOWING INSIDE OUT

🌐 www.zyzvennaturals.com

📍 167-169 Great Portland Street, Fifth Floor,
London, W1W 5PF, United Kingdom

SCAN

www.getnafi.com

167-169 Great Portland Street, Fifth Floor, London, W1W 5PF, United Kingdom

Kamila Aletha Atherley
Nurturing Hearts and Families Through Innovative Care

"Stay focused and refuse to go back into your comfort zone. Your business will be a success once you believe in yourself. Sometimes, you are all you have, so trust the process."

I have always been an outgoing person who is upfront with every individual I interact with. Additionally, I believe that it is always important to bless those less fortunate, so from as long as I can remember, I have often put together packages, which consist of food, clothing, and school supplies for the children of those who are unable to afford to provide for themselves and their families.

Working as a nurse for the last 16 years, I have been positioned to see the difficulties that people face when they come into the hospital for overnight and longer stays. Oftentimes, people are unprepared. The affected group that I found most interesting were expecting mothers, who would come to the hospital with nothing for their babies or themselves. Once they gave birth, they wouldn't have what they needed. In the many years that I have worked in the hospital setting, there were times when some of these individuals simply couldn't afford to supply their own needs because of their lack of resources, and I would help by giving what I could.

Then, at the height of the COVID-19 pandemic, more and more women started coming to the hospital not having the essential items needed or required for labour and delivery. Guyana was on lockdown like the rest of the world, and families simply couldn't access what they needed. For those who could afford to, whether or not there was a national lockdown, they needed to be able to purchase the necessary items. So, in July 2020, I decided to start a business to fill this gap; then Mila's Baby and ME Pre-Packed Maternity Bags was born.

I believe that I chose the right time to launch my business as the world was being instructed to practice social distancing, and as such, many expectant mothers in Guyana were elated to learn of the service I was providing. It relieved their fears of the impact that COVID-19 would have on them and their expected bundle of joy if they had to personally go into stores to procure these essentials themselves.

I created a business that continues to suit the budgets and wallets of the maternal community as well as their friends and family who wish to purchase packages as gifts for them. I started out with three types of packages; Standard pre-packed maternity bag for public and private hospitals, the Deluxe pre-packed maternity bag, and an Economy pre-packed maternity bag for those who are not as financially strong.

Later, I decided to add Partial packages, which cater to mothers-to-be, who just need a few things they are unable to source themselves. These are often purchased as gifts by friends, relatives, and co-workers. They have been a huge hit for baby shower goers. In keeping with the COVID-19 guidelines, I added complimentary sanitizer and face masks to each order. When I saw the need to cater to a wider market, I also started offering a 'build your own bag' package. These are specifically targeted at expectant mothers who require caesarean section and, therefore, need to be hospitalized for a longer period than mothers who deliver naturally.

Understanding that not all new parents have the knowhow when it comes to looking after themselves and their newborns postpartum, I also decided to add a booklet that I had specifically and personally designed and published for both expectant mothers and fathers. The booklet contains information from credible sources on important facts needed for parents to be prepared to take care of both mommy and baby, from the best positions for breastfeeding to how to properly clean the baby's umbilical cord to prevent infections along with other vital information. Over the years, this booklet has been updated as new information emerges, allowing me to ensure that my customers have the right information as needed.

I think that it is important, so I ask my clients as many questions as necessary in order to cater to their specific needs. No two mothers are the same, and I ensure that they feel seen and heard when I help each of them. For example, when providing advice about breastfeeding, I ensure that I consider what is comfortable for the individual mother. The same goes for when I am selling a pre-packed bag; I ensure that I focus on what the mother actually needs as opposed to selling them the biggest package that they do not necessarily need. Their satisfaction is what matters most to me. The most satisfying part of the service I provide is seeing how comforted a scared expectant mother becomes when I guide them along their journey and provide information that help them along the way.

Starting this business, I received a lot of support from my immediate family and a few friends in the forms of advice and advertising my business. However, nothing in this life comes without its challenges. To begin with, as I am a nurse attached to the public hospital, I was not allowed to conduct business in the hospital — the space where most of my clients are found, especially those who come in without the essentials for them and their babies. This was a challenge that I could not overcome. However, I didn't let that stop me. I accepted that those are the rules and sought out finding my clients in different ways. Sure, it would increase sales if I had access to this clientele, but there are many other ways to find my clients and they have been successful to a great extent.

One of the biggest challenges that I have faced in my business is unhealthy competition. If you are going into business, please understand that there will always be competition. It cannot be avoided, and it is healthy. However, I faced what I call unhealthy competition. There was one person who was following my page on social media and decided to start a business like mine. This would not have been a problem if she had not copied and pasted every aspect of my business. I don't mean that she stole one idea or product; she literally created a business that looked exactly like mine. She made no changes to make it unique to her in any way. To add insult to injury, she was also making the claim that she was the first to bring the initiative to our country, which clearly was a lie. My business had been featured in two of our national newspapers, The Guyana Chronicle and the Stabroek, which gained my business more exposure and also exposed the 'competition.' This was vindication but I still had to deal with my business idea being used by someone else.

Then there was another lady who also decided to copy my business idea. She had come to an event where I was selling my packages and came over to look at my products. Soon after, she was selling the exact same packages that I had on offer. I went to a pop-up event where she was. She heard that I was also going to be at the event and decided not to sell any packages on that day.

As you can imagine, it was extremely difficult dealing with this kind of 'competition.' Luckily for me, though, I have a good support system and people who reminded me constantly that these individuals were not me and could not do the exact same things that I would do to grow my business. This helped a lot. Since then, I have implemented a lot of new things in my business and has seen how much it has impacted it positively. The business is growing because of these changes, now taking Mila into the global market.

These weren't my only challenges, however. After a few months of running the business and seeing its success, I decided to apply for a business loan. I wanted to offer more to my clients and didn't have the money to do it. Now, if you have never tried to, let me tell you that it is a tedious process. Having success doesn't matter if you do not have financial progressions, a business plan, and so much more. I did not have quite a few of the many things they require. I just knew how to do what I was doing and it was working. When I was denied the business loan, I decided to take a personal loan to finance the business. I didn't want the lack of funds to deter me from the well-needed expansion.

Starting this business with my own money and being a single parent was beginning to take a toll on me in every way after the surge of COVID-19. With more people being able to go out to buy what they needed, sales dropped significantly, which affected the business' profits for a few months. I allowed fear to take its hold on me and became frustrated. I both wanted and attempted to give up several times. I was even encouraged to give up by some of the people around me. I had one person close to me tell me to shut the business down. Luckily for me, my family, especially my son, was very understanding and supportive of my business venture and encouraged me to not give up. I had taken out the loan and made the investment in myself, so I couldn't simply give up. It meant that I had to figure out how to keep the business in profit; I decided to 'up my game' and provide new offers to persons looking to purchase from my business.

I have since included more products to my business offerings. I have added a midwife service, which my clients love. I am even in the process of adding more categories and exciting services and offers. I have learned so much since July 2020 and continue to learn and grow as an entrepreneur. My wish for the future is to not only have a hugely successful business but to also use my business to sensitize people on the joys, dangers, and fulfilment of motherhood. I don't believe that enough emphasis is made on the journey to or of motherhood. Women on the whole suffer through a lot of different things on a physical and emotional level that needs to be highlighted, and if I can do so using my business as my platform, I will feel a sense of accomplishment.

My advice to all women in business, whether you are just starting out or in a place where your business is not bringing in the revenue you would like it to, is to not give up hope. Your challenges are meant to help you and your business grow. Competition has allowed me to challenge myself and diversify my business, which continues to lengthen the business' lifespan. Competition helps to keep you on your toes and pushes you to think outside the box, so welcome it. God did not put that idea into your mind for no reason. Keep praying and persisting. Stay focused and refuse to go back into your comfort zone.

Your business will be a success once you believe in yourself. Sometimes, you are all you have, so trust the process.

Who is she?

Kamila Aletha Atherley is a nurse and has been for over sixteen years. She's a natural caregiver, who has often come up with ideas to help others in her community. Considerate of the challenges that indigenous peoples in Guyana face, she aims to play her role in mitigating those challenges. Kamila has always cared about the wellbeing of baby and mother pre- and post-childbirth. This first led her to creating a booklet that would help parents by teaching them how to carry out different duties in looking after their newborns.

Then, in 2020, she saw a gap in the market — a need to ensure that those coming to the hospital had all they needed for their new baby — and started her business, Mila's Baby and ME Pre-Packed Maternity Bags. The business provides a unique service of pre-packed maternity bags to expectant mothers as well as customized baby shower gifts, games, and advice to both mother and father. Mila's bags can be ordered by expectant mothers and/or fathers or even as gifts for someone you care about. Kamila customizes each bag to suit her customers' needs and their pockets alike, ensuring that they are completely satisfied with each order they receive.

Today, Kamila continues to diversify her business offerings to meet the needs of the market. With many plans in the pipeline and upcoming launches, she's looking forward to taking her business internationally in the near future.

"If you are going into business, please understand that there will always be competition."
- **Kamila Aletha Atherley**

Christina Brooks
Lead with Conviction

"Silence self-doubt and shatter limiting narratives. Embrace your voice, raise your hand, and assert your presence. Our forebearers' struggles demand more than survival; they beckon us to flourish, to construct a world that mirrors our ideals, ambitions, and aspirations."

One of the most impactful challenges I've encountered revolves around my sense of belonging and self-worth. I've always aspired to learn, improve, and excel, regardless of the context — be it business, work, or personal life. However, a persistent hurdle has been the perception of not measuring up.

When I reflect on the leaders in the business world, I couldn't find anyone who resembled me. Within every organization I worked, there was no role model or member of the leadership team who made me feel that I rightfully belonged among them. Despite my unyielding determination and relentless desire for growth, this absence of relatable representation weighed heavily on me. I held the belief that I would need to carve my own path forward.

Throughout this journey, I grappled with an ongoing feeling of inadequacy. I never truly believed I was 'good enough.' In fact, I was forced to compartmentalize my identity. To fit into various professional situations, I presented only a fraction of my true self, adapting my persona to suit what I perceived as acceptable for the given audience.

The notion of bringing my authentic self to work felt like a luxury I couldn't afford. Instead, I meticulously curated a persona to align with the expectations of my surroundings. This involved concealing parts of my background, like not mentioning that I hailed from Tottenham (one of the poorest urban neighbourhoods in London) as it seemed to diminish my chances of callbacks. I often shifted my address along the Victoria line to seem more appealing to potential employers.

This façade persisted until I had the opportunity to establish my own organization. As I built this venture, I realized that authenticity was not just a preference; it was a necessity. The organization's success hinged on my ability to be genuine, to remove the barriers I had crafted over time. I recognized that I embodied the very issues my business aimed to address.

Embracing my authentic self became a pivotal turning point. It marked the transformation from fractured presentations to a cohesive, purpose-driven identity. This shift allowed me to lead with conviction, merging all aspects of who I am — the strengths, flaws, and complexities. It was through this metamorphosis that my business found its true essence and purpose.

Undoubtedly, this journey has been defined by the challenge of feeling out of place within various environments. However, this challenge has ultimately fuelled my determination to craft a space where authenticity thrives. By confronting my own struggles head-on, I've been able to pave the way for a more inclusive and genuine approach to leadership and business. It has shaped my perspective on leadership, authenticity, and the transformative power of embracing one's true self in the professional realm.

Overcoming this significant challenge required me to establish my own organization. The prevailing professional landscape seemed resistant to change, and the concept of authenticity often had subtle underlying restrictions. Rather than genuinely embracing every facet of oneself, the prevailing sentiment appeared to favour conforming to socially acceptable norms. The idea of "bringing your whole self to work" often translated into bringing only those parts that aligned with the established norms, while discarding the rest.

A pivotal moment in my journey came during my time at Rolls-Royce, a period that spanned approximately three and a half years. I had a can-do attitude and just would not take no for an answer. No problem was too big or small, which proved transformational with the executive leadership team. Having this acknowledgement validated my worth and the unique contributions I could make. I developed a close partnership with influential figures like the Chief People Officer, the HR Director, and the Director who initially hired me, even after I revealed that I was pregnant during the interview. This was a critical turning point where acceptance and value were demonstrated despite common narratives where women often faced challenges due to pregnancy.

In my leadership journey, gaining permission not just from others but from myself became an essential component. I recognized the necessity of permitting myself to fail, to take risks, and to venture into uncharted territories. This shift in perspective, akin to the mindset celebrated in cultures like the United States, fostered an environment where trying and failing were seen as brave acts of innovation, rather than grounds for harsh judgment. It was this mindset that my experiences at Rolls-Royce nurtured.

Regarding the question of how a challenge I faced fuelled my entrepreneurial journey, building my own business around my core values, vision, and mission became the ultimate solution. This approach aligned with my belief that true authenticity and self-expression thrive when ownership is claimed. By establishing an entity tailored to my perspective and goals, I liberated myself from subscribing to external values that clashed with my own. The corporate world, whether large or small organizations, often demands alignment with their predefined values. When this alignment is absent, a dissonance emerges, leading to feelings of discontent and energy drain.

Especially in the wake of events since 2020, a growing number of black entrepreneurs and leaders, like me, have chosen to step away from traditional corporate structures. The desire to avoid conforming to outdated paradigms has fuelled a surge in black-owned businesses. This movement represents a paradigm shift where individuals are taking control of their narratives, building ventures that are a true reflection of their values, and contributing to a more innovative, inclusive, and forward-looking business landscape.

As Black women, when it comes to starting your own business or ensuring its survival, you will face challenges. It is a given. However, success is also attainable. One of my cherished quotes defines success as the convergence of preparation and opportunity, with money being ancillary to this equation. The core of any business idea rests on your purpose and passion. So, my advice to young Black women, and young women in general, is this: Engage in work that resonates so deeply with you that you'd willingly do it without financial compensation. Seek roles, activities, and endeavours that truly nurture and fulfil you. This is where you should invest your energy.

Next, embrace the power of your network. Remember, your network isn't just a collection of connections; it's a dynamic asset that shapes your potential success. People within your network can pave the way, clear obstacles, and champion your cause. It's often said that your network is your net worth. Don't underestimate the ability of individuals to rally behind you and your aspirations.

Reflecting on my own journey, I started my executive search firm with a mere £5,000. In hindsight, even less could have sufficed. The essence of what I needed boiled down to a phone and good internet connection. Day in and day out, I found myself offering guidance, coaching, and support to others. This inherent inclination towards service laid the foundation for my business. I helped individuals recognize their innate strengths, aligning their lives with their true passions and abilities. This is the essence of success — finding your superpower, the skill that comes naturally to you but eludes others. It's your unique contribution to the world.

When you're motivated by your passion and purpose, money takes a back seat. It becomes the byproduct of your dedication rather than the initial driver. The journey starts with identifying what you truly care about and finding ways to impact the world in a meaningful manner. Money follows purpose and value, not the other way around.

While there are essential structural elements and governance considerations for scaling a business, these should never be the starting point. Avoid fixating on making a certain amount of money, as that mindset often stifles your authentic aspirations. Instead, focus on the legacy you want to leave, the impact you aim to create, and the positive change you can contribute to the world.

Remember, the pursuit of your passion, purpose, and impact will magnetize people towards you. Those who share your values and vision will be drawn to collaborate and invest, both emotionally and financially. Capitalizing on these intrinsic motivators will propel you forward, opening doors that you might never have imagined.

A word of advice: There will likely always be challenges that you face in your business, regardless of how established and successful it becomes. What matters is how you navigate those challenges. In my own company, we have overcome but continue to face challenges. Our business operates as a talent consultancy encompassing recruitment, diversity and inclusion, and consultancy services. Our unique approach is rooted in not only attracting talent but also ensuring their retention and development within organizations. Post-2020, many companies express the desire for greater diversity and inclusion, but we're committed to also examining the lived experiences of individuals once they're integrated into these environments. This holistic perspective is crucial to foster genuine change.

The challenges we encounter often mirror global market dynamics. For instance, when the COVID-19 pandemic hit, it posed a significant hurdle. Additionally, situations such as energy crises or international conflicts, like the war in Russia and Ukraine, create market uncertainties that impact our operations. In these circumstances, many global organizations tend to freeze hiring or postpone developmental initiatives, directly affecting our work.

However, I personally avoid consuming news, as my belief is that there's an inherent abundance of wealth in our world. The media often portrays a different reality than the conversations I have with clients and individuals. This perspective helps us maintain focus and drive regardless of external factors. While media influences people's perceptions and actions, I choose not to be swayed by it.

As a business, we continue to engage with clients and provide our services. We remain committed to our purpose. Instead of getting bogged down by the negative sentiments prevalent in certain markets, we expand our outlook to Commonwealth countries and global markets. For instance, if the narrative in one region is scarcity, we explore opportunities in regions experiencing growth.

I am unwavering in my conviction to not let media or market fluctuations dictate our business success. Even when the majority of the market seems to be in a downturn, we recognize that this might not be the case everywhere. By being agile and visionary, we're able to anticipate shifts and adapt our strategies accordingly. This approach allows us to stay ahead of the curve and not be confined by mainstream narratives.

Thus, my suggestion is that you turn to your own strengths when you face challenges in your business as they can often help you find solutions. My upbringing, for example, has played a significant role in shaping my approach to business and my advocacy for a different way of operating. From a young age, around seven or eight years old, my brother and I started a car washing business to address a gap we identified in our neighbourhood. This early inclination to solve problems and create opportunities laid the foundation for my entrepreneurial mindset.

Growing up, we faced financial challenges. My mother, despite limited means, managed to instil in us a sense of excitement and resourcefulness in the face of scarcity. As well as wash cars for neighbours, we would create games and puzzles to sell to other kids on the street. This upbringing reframed our perspective on having less and taught us how to innovate and create value with limited resources.

I remember collecting coupons and using stamps from the post office to get basic necessities like bread and milk. My mother transformed these experiences into engaging challenges, masking the financial limitations we were navigating. Her resourcefulness and creativity made us feel empowered rather than constrained.

This mindset of resilience and resourcefulness influenced me deeply. At the age of 15, I started working to contribute financially to our household and help with the mortgage, enabling us to keep our home. My mother's determination to maintain our property played a pivotal role in securing stability for us. Consequently, ownership emerged as a critical concept in my life. My mother, despite having very little, owned a property. At 21, I purchased a house, inspired by her example. I recognized the power of having assets and owning property, which solidified my belief in the importance of ownership as a means of securing one's future.

This perspective extends to my business philosophy. I firmly believe that creating and owning our businesses is a way to shape our own destinies and build structures that align with our values and aspirations. Many existing corporate structures were not designed for us; they may have been built by us, but not for our benefit. The historical legacy of certain industries and organizations, tied to exploitation and oppression, underscores the urgency for change.

My commitment to conscious leadership, conscious capitalism, and advocacy for the triple bottom line — people, planet, and profit — reflects my desire to disrupt existing systems and build a new paradigm. As a B Corp, my organization aligns with this charter and prioritizes a more inclusive and holistic approach to business. This is my response to dismantling outdated structures and constructing something that benefits the majority and promotes ethical practices.

To the young Black women who might be hesitating or uncertain about pursuing their dreams and entrepreneurial aspirations, I want to convey a message that resonates deeply with our current historical context. We find ourselves in a remarkable era where the very fabric of our environment and infrastructure is aligned to support our success.

This assertion is grounded in the transformative impact of recent events, especially the outbreak of COVID-19.

Never before have we witnessed such a powerful leveller as the pandemic, which brought together all communities, races, and individuals in the face of a common enemy. This global experience dissolved distinctions of black and white, rich and poor, unifying us in a shared struggle against the virus. This monumental event was followed by another transformative incident; the tragic murder of a Black man in the United States.

What sets this incident apart is its timing, occurring amid the ongoing aftermath of the pandemic. This convergence created a unique platform for our experiences and stories to resonate beyond racial lines. It was a time when everyone was willing to listen and understand, transcending historical biases.

For young Black women, this juncture holds immense significance. We stand on the cusp of an era where our voices can reverberate through our own platforms, liberated from the constraints of traditional media. YouTube, Snapchat, Instagram — these platforms empower us to shape narratives that reflect our unique perspectives and experiences.

The crucial lesson to internalize is that success isn't contingent on external factors; it's a product of our self-belief and determination. If you doubt your capacity, remind yourself that the only thing holding you back is your own perception of your limitations. Opportunities abound; it's your faith in your ideas, your preparedness, and your ability to seize those opportunities that truly define success.

I understand that fear can be a paralyzing force. I've encountered my share of it, particularly in the realm of public speaking. My upbringing, rooted in a Jamaican household with religious values, encouraged me to remain unobtrusive and reserved. But my message, my purpose, was far larger than my personal fears. It's a message that serves the community, echoes the struggles of the past, and envisions a future where our voices are celebrated.

It's easy to believe that success is a distant dream, that those who've been in business for years have an inherent advantage. But understand that I grappled with overwhelming fear too. I recall attending a leadership course at Windsor Castle, overcome with a sense of inadequacy among a diverse group. Yet, I realized my mission was transcendent — it went beyond me, encompassing the community, the ancestors, and generations yet to come.

Consider this: our ancestors could never have envisioned us here, expressing our thoughts on platforms like this. They endured unimaginable hardships to pave this path for us. Dismissing this moment, failing to advocate for our dreams, would diminish their sacrifices and dishonour our shared heritage.

So, I implore you to silence self-doubt and shatter limiting narratives. Embrace your voice, raise your hand, and assert your presence. Our forebearers' struggles demand more than survival; they beckon us to flourish, to construct a world that mirrors our ideals, ambitions, and aspirations.

My passion for this message extends far beyond my own individual journey. It serves as a guiding force, a touchstone that I can always return to. But it's not just about me; it's about our people, our community, and the legacy of our ancestors. To neglect speaking out, presenting my thoughts, or participating in panels would be an injustice to those who came before us. Their sacrifices, toil, and struggles laid the groundwork for us to stand here today. Five generations ago, they toiled in fields, dreaming of a world where women like you and I could share this message with the world.

It's imperative to acknowledge this responsibility and not let their efforts be in vain. When I consider the hardships they endured to pave the path we walk, it becomes clear that this duty transcends my personal ambitions. This perspective infuses purpose into my message and underscores why I carry it forward. As we sit at tables of influence, as we engage with institutions like Downing Street and the House of Lords, I recognize that these opportunities are a result of their collective struggle. My voice is their voice, and I'm compelled to speak on their behalf.

To young women starting out on their journeys, whether it's launching a business or taking on a significant career move, my advice is simple: take that step, even when you don't feel fully prepared. The truth is: nobody ever feels entirely ready. It's akin to parenthood or relationships — there's never a perfect time. The key is to step forward, embrace discomfort, and inhabit the future version of yourself you envision. I perpetually think about my future self, always planning for what lies ahead, even if it's years down the line. Breathing life into those aspirations is what propels me forward, and you can do the same.

Interestingly, I'm also part of a global leaders forum led by Baroness Verma, a UN delegate. We focus on Commonwealth countries, particularly women of colour, including those of Black heritage. This global perspective is crucial; we can't be confined to localized thinking. We must learn from various communities and cultures, adopting strategies that transcend borders. While some communities reach back to uplift their peers, our community often remains segmented. We need to change that narrative.

Addressing another topic, our relationship with money within the Black community has unique dynamics. We tend to shy away from conversations about credit, debt, borrowing, and lending. However, this reluctance limits our growth potential. We can learn from other communities that strategically leverage financial tools like borrowing to invest in their ideas. By reshaping our perspectives on money, we can empower ourselves and our ventures for greater success. It's a step towards dismantling the barriers that hold us back and embracing the full scope of our potential.

Who is she?

Christina is the Founder and CEO of Ruebik, a leading talent attraction agency, which specialises in recruitment and inclusion consultancy. As a life-long diversity inclusion advocate, her mission at Ruebik is to impart her knowledge and lived experiences to help better the lives of the disenfranchised, encompassing social mobility, gender, ethnicity, and disability.

She has over 20 years' experience in the talent attraction field, including Global Executive Talent Lead at Rolls-Royce, with executive search roots in investment banking and private equity. Through her extensive exposure to different industries and the motivations of business, Christina is adept in navigating the cultural and racial impacts on business, including boardroom and executive leadership roles.

Her passion in the field of equity and inclusion is further reflected in her personal endeavours. She is a Trustee for an alternative provision school in Tottenham, a mentor to incarcerated youth, and advisor to Black-owned social start-ups.

"Take that step, even when you don't feel fully prepared."
- **Christina Brooks**

I am NOT limited by:

My ethnicity
My sexual orientation
My religion
My gender

Your judgement.

Empowering people from diverse backgrounds is one thing. Providing opportunities for these accomplished professionals with extraordinary potential, is quite another. Welcome to Ruebik. A leading talent attraction agency, where skill and expertise always come first. It is our pledge to transform the profile of decision makers and to educate organisations on the value of leading with inclusion.

🌐 www.ruebik.com
📍 London, United Kingdom
📞 0208 058 6968

Kemone S-G Brown-Tshabalala

Every Problem has a Solution; Find it

"If you employ people whose values do not align with yours, you will have to be willing to change, let them bring your business to the ground, or let them go at some point. Those are the choices that you will have."

I think I'll have to start off with the first and probably most important lesson that I want to leave you with: Every business, every individual, no matter their success, have faced or are currently facing challenges. No one has it made. I mean that. Not even the person who was born with a supposed silver spoon in their mouth. The reality is that we are often just faced with different challenges. Now, it doesn't matter how big or small a problem is; a problem is a problem, and problems require solutions.

I wanted to get that out of the way, because too often, whether as businesswomen, aspiring businesswomen, or just women, we think that a problem that we face is the biggest mountain to ever exist. In my opinion, this kind of thinking gets in our way far more than any problem that we face. Now, the other part of this is that we often think that the person who is doing well in their business: (1) has it all together; (2) is not faced with challenges; and (3) just haven't faced any of the problems that we have.

I believe that I have removed point two from the discussion already, but let me reiterate by saying everyone faces challenges. As for point one, no one ever has it all together. Some of us just know how to keep it together on the outside better. Finally, in my opinion, there isn't a problem that exists that has not been faced by someone else yet. The world is too big of a place for us to be the only one who's been through what we are going through. There are too many variables to consider, which I think makes that physically impossible. You might be the first to speak about having the problem on the internet but being the first or only to face it, I think, is impossible or very close to it.

I know these are all very bold statements, but I don't want you to get hung upon them. In actuality, it's just my opinion, but if you think about it deeply, you'll probably come to the same conclusion.

Now that we've got that out of the way, I want to talk about myself as an entrepreneur and some of the challenges that I've faced, overcome, and learned from. First, though, I want to tell you a little bit about myself. I grew up in Jamaica where, as a young dark skinned girl, not a lot seemed accessible to me. From arguments with my sisters where I'd be told that I'm "black like tar" to not being liked or paid much attention to by my teachers, I've always known that the colour of my skin could be a hindrance to who and what I became when I grew up. So, from a very young age, where I would fit into society has been at the forefront of my mind to some extent.

Unfortunately, the world around me was not prepared for the person I was on the inside. I have never been that child to stand back and hold a place given to me when it wasn't a place that I wanted to be in. I was that child who spoke up for what she believed in, no matter the consequences. Whether you would discipline me, not talk to me, or whatever you decided, it held no bearing on me claiming my space. I always believed that I could do and be anything that I wanted to be, and no one was going to get in the way of that.

Luckily for me, during my childhood, when I was bullied for the tone of my skin, the thickness of my hair, the size of my eyes, the loudness of my voice, my father instilled in me the belief that my 'blackness' was not a weakness but a source of strength, beauty, and heritage. He continuously reminded me of my worth and beauty, a sentiment he still echoes during our video calls. A firm believer in the power of education, he repeatedly emphasized that excelling in school was my ticket out of our neighbourhood. He'd often say, "If you do well in school, you can escape this place." These teachings helped me to be strong and resilient in more ways than anyone could have ever imagined. I have faced abuse, poverty, and so much more. I fought against the system that was meant to keep me in my place, broke free from poverty, and created a world for myself that people where I come from often don't even know that exists.

By the time I reached the age of 11, I found myself wrestling with the questions posed by teachers about my future aspirations. I often provided the conventional responses, as they sounded impressive. However, deep down, I harboured no desire to become a nurse, lawyer, or doctor. My ultimate goal was remarkably straightforward: I wanted to make money, make a difference in the world, and be free while doing it. The driving force within me was not tethered to a specific profession. I lacked that intrinsic pull toward any particular career path. I realised that I was good at and liked many things and I did not want to be tied to any one thing. Consequently, I decided to excel in all my subjects, recognizing that specialization could limit my options. Whether it was the sciences, business, or the arts, I embraced each subject wholeheartedly. This commitment to learning became a hallmark of my entire life's journey, a testament to my ability to do pretty much anything and give it my best.

I also vividly recall a critical moment when I discerned a stark difference between my parents' daily routines and decided that I wanted something better for myself. I wanted the kind of freedom I hadn't necessarily witnessed yet but somehow knew existed. While my mother diligently went to work each day, she struggled to make ends meet. In contrast, when my father lived with us and toiled day in and day out, he consistently brought home money, and we never went without. This discrepancy made me realize that my mother was dependent on her job, relying on someone else to provide her with income, hence the waiting period for her pay checks. On the other hand, my dad, as a self-employed auto mechanic, took charge of his earnings. He determined that he would make money every day and ensured it benefitted our family. I knew then that I wanted to be my own boss and run my own business but I needed to build myself up to the point where I would be able to do that. I learned very late in life about funding opportunities and how the world of money worked, so in my mind, I was just going to have to work, save capital, and go off to start my own business.

Now, as I got older and started getting closer to entering the world of work, I became more concerned about my skin tone being a potential hindrance to accessing better job opportunities and freedom. Even during my school years, despite consistently excelling in my studies, I often felt overlooked by my teachers. It was disheartening to witness how some of my classmates with lighter complexions or curlier hair would receive excessive praise for their achievements, while my own accomplishments went largely unnoticed. Reflecting on this now still stirs emotions within me, as it bothered me for a significant portion of my life.

I want to clarify that I've always been proud of my skin tone. My father instilled in me, long before I attended primary school, that Black is undeniably beautiful. However, it was disheartening to witness society's failure to celebrate my achievements simply because I didn't conform to their predefined standards of what beauty or even good looked like. I reached a turning point at some indistinct moment in my journey when I decided to stop caring. I lacked positive female role models who celebrated the beautiful shade of my skin, but there was this one remarkable teacher during my tenth-grade year, who, like me, was of dark complexion. She taught literature, and in one of our classes, she delved into the saying, "If you're white, you're right. If you're yellow, you're mellow. If you're brown, stick around. But if you're black, get back."

Something profound shifted within me that day. Despite having heard numerous times that I was "black like tar," this phrase took the negativity to another level. There was no way society was going to dictate that I should step back simply because of my dark skin. Not a chance. I decided that I would unleash every ounce of my potential and lead life on my own terms. I vowed to speak up until my voice was heard, to choose the rooms I stood in, and to embrace every aspect of life to its fullest. As a Black, dark-skinned girl, I was determined to show the world just how Black and beautiful I truly am.

It was abundantly clear that embodying the qualities of Black and beautiful wouldn't automatically reshape the world around me. As I approached the end of my high school journey, my plan was to secure a job instead of immediately enrolling in college. I had spent my entire life up to that point carefully observing how things worked for individuals like me. I knew I couldn't bear the confines and limitations that life might impose. However, the reality I encountered was far more frightening than I had anticipated.

I read a job advert in the newspaper in my final year of school and thought that it would be a good test run. It was an opportunity to work after school on Friday evenings and on Saturdays. It would have been perfect. I was young, wore the clothes size of a model, and it was a job opening at a hotel that seemed tailor-made for someone with my body type, height, and skillset. I met with two gentlemen and a lady during the interview process, two of whom were White, and the other had fair skin. They were clearly impressed with me and were eager for me to start the very next day. They particularly admired my voice, deeming it the highlight of the interview. There would be no delays in getting me started, as all the dresses I'd have to wear would fit perfectly.

However, as we were leaving the interview, we crossed paths with a dark-skinned lady, whom I presumed to be one of the managers. She reacted with laughter when she learned that I had been chosen for the position. Her exact words still echo in my memory; she said they'd "only be able to see her teeth in the dark if the lights go out." In her eyes, I was too dark for the role. This incident marked my inaugural encounter with the harsh realities of the working world.

In response, I expressed my gratitude to the three interviewers for the opportunity but firmly declined the job offer. Why would I subject myself to working under the supervision of someone who saw me as less than who I was? I told myself that I deserved better, that I was far superior to her with her self-hate, and that I wouldn't willingly associate myself with anyone who didn't appreciate my true worth. This experience ignited a fire within me, reinforcing my commitment to never remain where I wasn't genuinely wanted. I held my self-worth in such high regard that I refused to subject myself to such mistreatment.

Now, throughout my life, I've always dabbled in various side hustles. It started at a young age when I realized I wanted my own money. I wanted to be able to buy things for myself and others, whether it was gifts for birthdays, Christmas, Mother's Day, or Teacher's Day, or simply going out with friends to the beach, movies, or the skating rink during holidays. So, I took it upon myself to find ways to earn my own money, and that's when I embarked on my first venture, doing people's hair. From that point on, I was determined to have multiple income streams.

As I grew older and completed high school, my desire to work intensified. I had excelled academically, passing all my subjects with flying colours, so I initially thought finding a job would be a breeze. However, reality proved otherwise. I found myself applying for jobs that required qualifications far less impressive than mine. I performed well in interviews but inexplicably didn't secure the positions. It became evident that not only was my skin tone a factor limiting my opportunities, but my address also played a significant role in the equation. I lived in 'the ghetto,' where many Jamaicans still believe 'nothing good comes from.' The moment I started lying about where I lived on my CV, I started getting more call backs; however, I would still be rejected when I turned up with my dark skin. That wasn't something I could leave at home and I wouldn't have wanted to.

Eventually, I did secure a job and swiftly ascended the ranks. Within months, I was a manager. My strong work ethic, commitment to customer satisfaction, and unique problem-solving abilities caught the attention of my employer, who appreciated my contributions. However, to my colleagues, my rapid advancement could only be attributed to a presumed relationship with the boss. I soon grew weary of dealing with the hostility and office politics and handed in my resignation.

Fortunately, I'd continued to pursue my side hustles diligently, providing me with a safety net.

It wasn't until I worked at the Bob Marley Museum that I experienced a workplace where I wasn't discriminated against due to my dark skin. It was the first job where I didn't encounter any insinuations or variations of "she's too dark." They hired me solely based on my competence to excel in the role. Although this experience showed me that not all companies in Jamaica held prejudiced views, I still believed that the world had more to offer than just working for someone else, even if it meant not settling for the relatively rare instances of fairness and equality in the job market.

My experiences with negative reactions to my skin took a different turn when I moved to South Africa. Here, I faced racism, not just colourism. There are too many incidents to share here, so I'll share one. I had been accepted into a specific university, received my acceptance letter with instructions of what to do next, and went to register for my courses. However, the lady assisting me seemed utterly shocked. She couldn't believe that the person standing before her, with the impressive grades on paper, was me. It was as if she needed confirmation, asking, "Are you sure you're Kemone Brown?" This encounter left me equally stunned. It was only later that I figured out why she was so baffled by my appearance. I was as Black as they came, but on paper, she thought I was Coloured because of my surname.

I realized that studying law, a subject built on opinions and interpretations, in an environment rife with discrimination would be an exhausting battle. I couldn't fathom waking up every day, fighting to prove my worth and demanding that others judge me based on my abilities, not the colour of my skin. So, I made a significant decision and opted to study mathematics instead. Mathematics offered a clear-cut world of right and wrong. There was no room for subjective judgments; solutions were either correct or incorrect, grounded in objective rules and principles.

My experiences with racism continued when I moved to England. During a job application with the Council, I faced racist treatment from a lady to the point that a White male applicant walked out of the exam just before I did, expressing his reluctance to work for such a prejudiced institution. Over the years, this workplace bias persisted. I even took on a lecturing position at a university in the UK, only to leave because my colleagues believed that I must have secured the job through improper means. I had no patience for such baseless accusations and hostilities when I could be using my time more productively.

That was the turning point for me. I had always known I would encounter challenges in life because of my skin, but this was the breaking point. Despite claims that slavery is over and the world is fair, the reality is different. So, I made a firm decision that enough was enough. I know I am unique, and I am aware of the value I bring to the table. I refuse to sell my skills and knowledge to individuals or companies that show no respect for me as a human being. It's not even enough for someone to say they like me as a Black person but dislike Black people in general because I am my people, connected to all my ancestors and brothers and sisters. I firmly decided, with the grace of God, that I would never work for someone else again because I have to. If ever I took a job with someone, it would be because I genuinely wanted to and felt comfortable enough around the people I was working with.

Now, when I take a moment to reflect on my entrepreneurial journey and all that has brought me to this point today, I'm reminded of numerous experiences and challenges that could fill an entire book. However, for the sake of brevity, I'll touch on just a few pivotal moments. This brings me to a crucial lesson I've learned in business, one that I believe every Black female entrepreneur should grasp early on: Not all money is good money. Some opportunities should be left on the table, untouched. I've come to understand that not all money is money I'm willing to accept. At the end of the day, I must ask myself, "Can I sleep peacefully at night?" I'd rather make £10 in a day than earn £100,000 if that £100,000 comes from unsavoury sources.

I have set clear boundaries for my business and myself. I cannot work with everyone, especially those whose values and beliefs not only differ from mine but also threaten my well-being as an individual. I refuse to knowingly accept money from someone who openly promotes racism. My business can thrive without such income.

When a client is rude or disrespectful to my staff to the point where it affects their well-being, I cannot, in good conscience, accept their money. Every person has value, and by taking that person's money while expecting my staff to carry out their work, I'd be conveying that money is more important than my team's dignity and well-being. That is something I'm not willing to be responsible for.

I've left substantial sums of money on the table, but I've never felt guilty about it. Our expenses are always covered, and I've never failed to pay my staff. I believe I'm doing something right, and I feel that there's a force looking out for me and my business.

To illustrate this further, consider a recent editing job we booked. The client initially seemed polite in our conversations and paid us a significant amount for the work, an amount that could have covered a substantial portion of someone's salary. However, as our editor started working on the project, it became evident that something was terribly wrong. When I asked, she wouldn't say what the problem was at first. Eventually, when I took her aside, thinking it was a personal issue, I found out that her problem was indeed work related. The document was saturated with racism, sexism, homophobia, and various forms of discrimination.

Our editor, a Black female, was deeply affected by the content. She felt conflicted, thinking it wasn't her place to take it personally and that her job was simply to edit the document. I couldn't allow her to go through the distress of editing a book that tore apart her identity. How could I ask her to help someone improve their writing when they were essentially telling her that she was insignificant as a human being? I promptly pulled her off the project and reached out to the client, explaining that we couldn't proceed with the edit. We issued a full refund and made it crystal clear that we do not support any form of discrimination and would not associate ourselves with such a book, even as editors.

It was my responsibility to take a stand, as both the well-being of my staff and my company's reputation were at stake. The money was not worth compromising our principles. As a Black-owned business, I could not support racism in any form. Even editing such content would have implied support, even if it was just "something I was getting paid to do."

I hope you'll take this lesson to heart: not all money is good money. You don't have to accept every opportunity that comes your way. In my view, this is a swift path to undermining your business and compromising your personal values. What's the point of endorsing something you don't believe in? There is no amount of money worth sacrificing your principles for. It's perfectly fine to say, "I'm sorry, I choose not to work with you." You don't have to work with everyone, and you certainly don't have to chase after every penny that's out there.

Another major challenge that I have faced in my business is human resources. Employing people is no easy feat when you are trying to build or maintain a business. In the past, I have employed both family and friends alike. Hence, I am not going to give you the cliché advice that you mustn't employ family and friends, because in all honesty, I do think that you can, and it can go well. In my experience, family and friends have not done as better or as worse when compared to the "strangers" I have hired.

Employing people I didn't know before hiring them also presented multiple challenges. Yes, they may be different but what remains the same is that they are problems that we face with human resources, regardless of who the individuals are. When there is work to be done, clients being let down because of human resources failure, because workers do not show up, it really doesn't matter who they are or what their reasons are. The problem remains the same.

So, what I am trying to say is that you are going to have many challenges when it comes to employing and working with people. It's part of the process. It won't always work out as you hoped it would. No matter what these problems are, you have to pick yourself up, analyse the situation, and find solutions. In my **Building Resilience in Your Business** course, I implore that the ultimate way to resolve your human resources issues is to Get Employment Right. Simply saying the solution is to not employ family and friends won't remove the challenges that you are bound to face. No matter who the person is, if a human being does not have good work ethics, if they do not share similar values to you and your business, it really doesn't matter who they are to you. If you employ people whose values do not align with yours, you will have to be willing to change, let them bring your business to the ground, or let them go at some point. Those are the choices that you will have.

For example, if you are a genuinely nice person who just wants everyone to play their part as you each get on with your work but people take that for granted, you must ask yourself whether you are willing to change. To become someone who is too strict, micromanages, and treat staff like they are just numbers. Are you willing to not be the nice guy because your staff continuously go against the values you hold and those of your company? If you don't want your staff to fear you; you want to go into work and feel relaxed as everyone gets on with it; then you must find people who value that as well.

Thus, in my perspective, the difference lies in aligning values and truly understanding potential. I've learned that I often believe in people more than they believe in themselves. I can recognize potential, even when individuals may not see it in themselves. This has led me to hiring individuals who don't necessarily align with my values or aren't where I need them to be at the moment. I sometimes think, "I can see their potential, and I can help them develop it." However, I've come to realize that it's crucial to shift this approach. Instead of focusing solely on potential, it's more effective to seek individuals who already understand their potential and are willing or eager to grow in the direction I'm heading. This is what works for my business and the culture that I aim to cultivate.

When it comes to friendships and relationships, we often talk about finding our tribe — those people we resonate with, connect with, and identify with. I think the same principle applies to hiring. Just like in personal relationships, you sometimes overlook red flags because you see other qualities you admire. However, if there's a major red flag, it might be wise to look elsewhere. There are people out there who possess the qualities you seek without those red flags.

Also keep in mind that hiring family and friends can jeopardize not only your professional relationships but also your personal ones. The same principles apply — just as there are family members or friends who wouldn't be a part of your life if they weren't related to you, there are also those who naturally fit into both your personal and professional worlds.

This lesson has significantly impacted my personal life and business decisions. For the sake of my business's success and my mental health, I've had to let go of personal relationships that didn't belong in my life. Having PMDD, experiencing depression, and dealing with anxiety have taught me the importance of maintaining a stress-free environment. These issues were exacerbated when certain people made life challenging, and it became clear that they didn't belong in my personal or professional life.

I need a life without stress or one-sided relationships, both personally and professionally. If I held onto those negative elements in my personal life, they would inevitably affect my business. Therefore, I made the conscious choice to clean up my personal life to ensure the well-being and success of my business. It's akin to a mourning period for the relationship because it's not just about letting go; it's also about moving forward.

As significant as those relationships were, reflecting on this journey, I don't find myself wishing I hadn't lost those relationships. Instead, I'm grateful because my personal life has improved by leaps and bounds. I'm now living a personal life I didn't even know was possible. Moreover, my business life has also seen remarkable improvements. I've shed the stress that used to plague my business — unhappy clients, my own unhappiness, and overall chaos. The positive transformation in both my personal and professional life is truly remarkable.

So, I advise you to approach employment with the right mindset. Don't categorically rule out hiring family or friends; it's not about who they are but about their ability to meet the expectations that you have for your business. Set boundaries and policies to ensure a fair working environment. More than anything else, listen to your gut feeling; it often tells you if someone is not the right fit for your team. Choosing the wrong people can indeed harm your business.

The other thing to consider with human resources is being prepared for anything that could happen. For instance, if you have a team of three employees, envision what could happen if one of them can't come to work on a specific day. Plan for contingencies to ensure the smooth operation of your business even in such situations. The resilience and adaptability of your business depend on how well you've prepared for these challenges.

I can share from my experience that my business, THP, has come a long way. We began working on it in 2019 and officially registered it as a limited company in 2022. During this journey, we've learned that having a smaller, quality team is more effective than a larger one. It's not about the number of staff you have; it's about having the right people in your team who align with your business's goals and values.

Don't be afraid to let go of individuals who do not respect your business or its values. Keeping people around simply because you need their specific skills or services, even if they repeatedly let you down, can hinder your business's growth. In the long run, it's detrimental to your business's identity and success.

Remember, running a business is not a casual activity or a hobby; it's a serious commitment. Treat it as such, and your team will follow suit. When your staff witnesses your dedication to maintaining a high standard of professionalism and integrity in your business, it helps shape the culture and identity of your company.

It's essential to understand that people, including employees, may occasionally disappoint you; it's a natural part of working with human beings. However, by being prepared and maintaining a strong commitment to your business's values, you can navigate these challenges effectively.

Now, as for the concern of people potentially stealing your business ideas, it's a common worry. I have had many staff leave and go off to start their own publishing or editing companies. It does not bother me by any means. They say, "Imitation is the sincerest form of flattery," and I do agree. I am always happy when I can motivate and inspire others. You should expect that others might see and even replicate your ideas, but this isn't necessarily a bad thing. Competition can be a positive force that drives innovation and growth. So, while it's natural to feel frustrated or disheartened when someone copies your concept, it's essential to keep several key points in mind.

Firstly, always remember that no one else can be you. Your unique perspective, skills, and passion are the driving forces behind your business. Even if others imitate your idea, they can never duplicate your essence or the personal touch you bring to your work. This distinctiveness is a valuable asset that sets you apart.

Consider this: If I had decided to close my business doors every time someone copied my idea, THP would not exist today as the thriving and progressive company it has become. Opening yourself up to sharing your business concept and strategies is essential if you want to leave a lasting legacy. While there's a risk that someone might copy your idea, it's outweighed by the rewards of building a meaningful legacy.

Don't enter this journey with the misconception that no one will ever try to copy your idea, because it might happen. Instead, focus on the bigger picture of leaving your mark in the business world. It's perfectly acceptable to discuss the inner workings of your business with others, and occasionally, someone might decide to mimic your idea. However, always bear in mind that they can never fully replicate your vision, insights, or the unique path that your business will take.

Now, one of the things that we don't talk about enough as Black women is our mental health. I have Pre-menstrual Dysphoric Disorder or PMDD. The simplest way to explain this is to say that it is like having PMS on steroids. When my PMDD is not under control, I can lose days or weeks of my life. It's crippling and robs me of every bit of joy that life has to offer. When I surrounded myself with the people who weren't good for my mental health, it affected me severely and my business suffered. I also suffer from depression, which seems to only be triggered by what is happening in my personal life. This meant that I had to clean up my personal life, and though it was one of the hardest things I've ever done, it has by far been the best gift I have ever given myself. I no longer have weeks when my business falls apart because

I cannot manage it. I no longer have weeks where I suffer from PMDD, where it takes over my life.

Therefore, my advice to you is to do what is necessary to preserve your mental health. Take time off if you need to. It's better for your business to fall apart than if you do. Entrepreneurship in itself means much more to me than just money; it's about freedom and self-discovery. Creating my own business reveals different facets of my identity and shows my capacity for anything and everything. There have been times in my life when my mental health was in tatters, and I couldn't get out of bed for days. However, because I've cultivated a risk-taking mentality, I know that I'll be alright even if I were to walk away from a business today, so I take time off when I need to.

Remove everything and everyone who brings chaos to your life and impact your life so negatively that you cannot be there for yourself. It will hurt at first, but when you start experiencing true peace and freedom, you will realise that it was well worth it. In the last two years, I have removed so many people from my life but I am living a life that I didn't even know existed. For the first time in my life, I know true peace. I know what it's like to not be surrounded by vampires who take and take, leaving me with absolutely nothing for myself.

Get into therapy if necessary. If you aren't well, you lose the ability to do things well. I have spent thousands of pounds looking after my mental health; therapy has been one of the best tools for me to draw on when I needed it and I know for a fact that it can help you if that is what you need. Invest in your own well-being. Look after your mental health and get help if you need it. You have to be doing well so that you can do everything else to the best of your ability.

While I love being an entrepreneur, I've also come to realize that I am not defined by my business; it doesn't make me who I am. I am more significant than any business venture, so I have to make myself a priority. By acknowledging my desires and pursuing them, I've ignited a fire within me that can never be extinguished. This fire sustains me through the toughest times, allowing me to take breaks, fall apart if needed, and then gather myself when I'm ready.

My journey as an entrepreneur is an affirmation of my desire for autonomy, freedom, and the pursuit of work that resonates with my passion and values. I don't believe in working solely for financial gain. I must feel connected and passionate about what I do; otherwise, I won't engage in it. I must also have the level of freedom that allows me to truly live and take part in life. My life cannot be consumed by my work. I recall being asked by a lecturer in university, what I would do after completing my degree. When I told him that I would only become a business owner because I refuse to be a slave, he was very offended. To him, I was calling him a slave for working his nine to five. I apologized but also wanted to clarify my perspective. My roots trace back to Jamaica, a place with a painful history of slavery. I believe this legacy goes beyond physical hardship; it also affects mental health and the sense of belonging. To be subjected to the rules and regulations of others, especially when it hinders your well-being, is something I wanted to avoid. I didn't want a life where I had to request time off for a holiday or a mental health break but be refused because I didn't have time left over from my allotted days off. I desired the freedom to choose when and how I worked, and entrepreneurship allows me that freedom.

Entrepreneurship, I've also realized, wasn't an escape from the complexities of human nature. It didn't shield me from racism or challenges. It was a journey filled with its own set of obstacles and trials. However, it provided me with the space to carve my own path, to challenge conventions, and to stand up for what I believe in. It offered me the freedom to confront the world on my own terms.

In my entrepreneurial journey, I've faced challenges, and it's been filled with ups and downs. Yet, it's a path I wouldn't trade for anything, as it has allowed me to embrace my true self and fight for the freedom I've always longed for.

When it comes to facing challenges in your entrepreneurial journey, it's important to take a step back and recognize that these challenges are an integral part of running a business. Embrace them as inherent aspects of your entrepreneurial path. As an aspiring entrepreneur, it's crucial to be prepared for every possible scenario and consider all potential challenges that may arise within your business. At the same time, remember that you cannot prepare for everything, so take heart, stand back, find solutions, and decide what your next steps will be when challenges come up. Every problem has a solution; you just have to find it.

Who is she?

Kemone S-G Brown-Tshabalala is simply multifaceted. She is an entrepreneur, researcher, public speaker, human rights activist, coach, trainer, and all round lover of life.

She is co-owner and the Managing Director at Tamarind Hill Press Limited, an independent publishing company, which also provides author services to the public, from book editing and book design to coaching authors through the writing process.

As a business coach, Kemone works with individuals to bring their business ideas to life from idea generation to launch. She has helped to launch over 30 successful businesses to date, and is presently busy helping others. She also helps established companies improve their internal and external communication strategies through a wide variety of training programs.

Naturally inquisitive, and given her background in mathematics and research, Kemone can often be found conducting research whether for one of her own projects or for a business she's been commissioned by. As if that's not enough to fill one person's day, Kemone is also an international keynote speaker, specialising in domestic abuse and violence, LGBT+ rights and life, women living with PMDD, Sexual and Reproductive Health and Rights (SRHR), HIV/Aids and lesbian and bisexual women, women's and children rights, and gender and equality.

Kemone is passionate about giving back and donates to individuals living in poverty and the charities that serve them. She believes that education is indeed the key to success and helps children in her native Jamaica, by donating to their education financially and through mentorship.

"There is no amount of money worth sacrificing your principles for."
- **Kemone S-G Brown-Tshabalala**

THP

TAMARiND HiLL
.PRESS
Independent Book Publisher

SCAN QR CODE FOR
10% OFF

PROFESSIONAL
AUTHOR
SERVICES & MORE

We have edited over 7000 documents to date, including emails, business proposals, theses, eBooks, and manuscripts. Over 95% of our clients rate our services as excellent, and 53% of our monthly service buyers are repeat customers.

ABOUT US:

Tamarind Hill Press Limited is an **independent book publishing company** based in County Durham, United Kingdom. We publish written works in English. THP is committed to bringing **high quality literary works** to the public through our in-house publishing and editing services; hence our slogan, "Changing the world one word at a time!" Additionally, we offer **business training** for Business Communication Enhancement, writer coaching and training, memoir writing, and much more.

- Book Publishing
- Ghost-writing
- Writer Training
- Book Editing
- Business Training
- English Enhancement

Newton Aycliffe Business Park, County Durham, DL5 6XP

CONTACT US

+44 1325 775 255
+44 7982 909 037

www.tamarindhillpress.com

Yushima Cherry-Burks

Empowering Survivor Healing and Advocacy

"Entrepreneurship can be demanding, and it's easy to fall into the trap of self-doubt or self-criticism when things don't go as planned. Embrace the fact that setbacks and challenges are part of the journey and an opportunity for growth. Allow yourself to learn from them, adjust your strategies, and keep moving forward."

I never expected to become a clinical therapist, an author, and owner of my own business. My business was born from pain and necessity; the formula for most inventions. If there is a need that hasn't been met, trust and believe a woman can and will find a way to make it happen. It's what we do. It's who we are.

My entrepreneurial fire was first lit by what my daughter went through.

When I looked into her big brown eyes, I knew something had changed within her. I questioned her, but she denied anything happening to her. I thought she may have been getting bullied by another child, but the truth was much worse than I could have ever imagined. I talked to the day-care owner about her recent change in behaviour, and she promised to keep an eye on things for me.

During this time, I had been contacting the Department of Human Services (DHR) once a year for five years. They investigated and the results were always the same — "unsubstantiated." The last time they investigated, the DHR worker locked eyes with me and said, "Look, lady, nothing happened to this little girl. You are wasting our time. If you contact us again, I will have you arrested and I will report that you are abusing your daughter." The very next year, I learned that my daughter had been sexually abused in that trusted family day-care. I felt alone and afraid, and that wasn't the first or the last time the system failed me, but I couldn't allow my fear to overpower my desire to gain justice for my daughter. I had a decision to make, even if that meant getting arrested.

Thankfully, I wasn't arrested, and my daughter finally disclosed what she experienced. I knew that she needed help. My focus went toward getting her therapy and understanding more about child abuse, sexual abuse, and my rights as a parent seeking help for her child. I needed to understand how this happened. I wanted to know the signs and symptoms of child abuse, so I learned the laws. I met with the local senators and representatives to introduce bills that would put in place stricter laws against predators and paedophiles. My life was consumed with protecting my child, our children, all children and families affected by child sexual abuse, directly and indirectly.

Twenty years ago, there were no support groups for victims or families affected by sexual abuse; in fact, that subject was taboo, and I could not find help anywhere. It took me two years of studying, learning, and working before I felt confident enough to teach our communities about the epidemic of secrets, games and guilt, and child sexual abuse. I emptied my bank account, opened an office space and started teaching our community, empowering children to disclose and parents to believe them.

I never intended for this to become my career; this career chose me. Twenty years later, I continue to help families heal from the trauma of abuse. My memoir, *Picking Up the Pieces to 100 Broken Promises*, tells the story of survival, disappointment, and overcoming the pain of people and systems that fail us. It also provides hope and shows the promises of God that we can stand on in the midst of chaos. *The Companion Workbook to Picking Up the Pieces to 100 Broken Promises* is a blueprint on how to begin the process of healing interpersonal trauma in practical ways. "T-Shirts and Tutu's" is a guide to heal our inner childhood trauma by addressing the little girl within us, and identifying what she needs (whatever your unmet needs and wants are, from tutu's to safety) then developing a plan of action to provide her with all of the things that she deserves.

My experience, education, and compassion for survivors of abuse motivates me to continue to find innovative ways to assist in the healing process. At Chatterbox Therapists, I offer individual counselling, couples counselling, premarital counselling, a dynamic parenting and co-parenting masterclass, workshops, and much more. I provide sessions virtually, and in-person, I am grateful for the ability to reach so many families.

Working with survivors has its challenges, hence, self-care has to be a priority. I learned this the hard way. As an advocate at heart, I had to learn how to set healthy boundaries, but I didn't know what I needed until I found myself in a place where I was depressed, while acting as though everything was fine. I was helping families rebuild their lives while mine was falling apart.

I had been taking care of people my whole life. As a child, I had to figure out my mother's needs before she knew them in order to keep the peace in our home. This caused me to develop a need to people please. I didn't know the difference between helping others and pleasing others until I was forced to begin the healing process for myself. Helping others empowers them to make the changes they need in their lives without my need to sacrifice myself, my time outside of business hours, or my emotional health and well-being. Helping others involves creating an environment where my clients own their feelings, emotions, wins, and losses. I am there to assist them in their need to process, without taking part in it myself.

Nothing made me angrier than setting a boundary and compromising that boundary for someone who didn't care or appreciate my sacrifice. I had to learn that no one is worthy of crossing my boundaries, no one's feelings are more important than my own, and no one's needs are more important than mine. That sounds selfish to someone who hasn't done the work or suffered as I have, I know. I also used to think this was absurd. It went against everything I had learned from childhood on. Once I realized that the people who taught me these toxic traits were the very ones benefitting from my lack of boundaries, it made me draw a hard line in the sand. I had a decision to make, and I decided to put my healing first.

Setting boundaries caused me to take pause and identify who I am as a woman first, what I need, where I fall short, and my strengths. I had to learn what I liked, the movies I wanted to watch, the way that I liked my eggs, the foods I wanted to eat, and so much more about myself. I didn't know any of these things because I always conformed to what everyone else around me wanted. I settled. I settled for whatever was available to me. This didn't reflect what I wanted for my life. I found myself questioning decisions I made. I needed confirmation from others that I was doing the right thing. I hadn't learned how to trust myself yet. When we grow up in abusive homes, we learn how to turn off our intuition in order to survive. We live in a constant state of fight or flight and until we tell the little girl and little boy inside of ourselves that we are safe, we remain in a heightened state of confusion, self-doubt, and self-destruction (directly and/or indirectly).

I needed to better understand myself in order to better serve my community. I needed to heal in order to fully enjoy my life. My smiles are authentic now and my interactions are genuine. My peace of mind came the moment I made a decision to put God and my needs first. I was able to do this because it's what He wanted for me. I had to realize that I am not a martyr for the cause. I am much more effective in the spaces where I operate in wellness. I was worried about what others would think of the new me. I learned that my clients were fine with my boundaries, my friends who wanted what was best for me understood that I couldn't make it to every event, and they stuck around even when I said "no." I had to let some people go, and while it hurt initially, it was like removing a tac from my shoe that I didn't know was there. I was no longer numb; I was happy, healthy, and whole.

My healing experience is not exclusive to me because I'm a therapist. It didn't just come to me, I had to search for it, fight for it, and want it more than anything. I had to learn that my business was my business, and not my life. My family was worthy of getting more than the left-over pieces of myself that I could muster up at the end of a long exhausting day. My clients deserved more than a therapist that could provide them with support, and comfort, but an example of what it looks like to be healed. I love this person and I want to help others love all of their pieces too!

I want to take a moment to acknowledge the challenges and difficulties you may be facing in your businesses. Building and growing a business is never an easy journey, and as women, we often encounter unique obstacles along the way, and as Black women, those obstacles may become barriers. However, I want to remind you of the incredible strength, resilience, and determination that resides within you.

First and foremost, please know that you are not alone. Many of us have faced similar hurdles and uncertainties, and it is through the support of our village that we can overcome them. Reach out to your fellow entrepreneurs, join communities, and seek mentorship from those who have walked this path before you. Surrounding yourself with your support system can provide valuable guidance, encouragement, and fresh perspectives.

Remember to be kind to yourself; give yourself grace. Entrepreneurship can be demanding, and it's easy to fall into the trap of self-doubt or self-criticism when things don't go as planned. Embrace the fact that setbacks and challenges are part of the journey and an opportunity for growth. Allow yourself to learn from them, adjust your strategies, and keep moving forward.

Don't hesitate to ask for help when you need it. It's okay to seek advice or delegate tasks that may be overwhelming, this will require letting go of the reigns, in order to hold on to your dreams. Recognize your strengths and areas where you may need additional support.

Building a strong team or seeking guidance from professionals can alleviate some of the burden and help you focus on what you do best.

Celebrate your successes, no matter how small they may seem. Recognize and appreciate the milestones you achieve along the way. Each step forward, each lesson learned, and each accomplishment is a testament to your resilience and hard work.

Lastly, believe in yourself and your vision. Trust that you have the skills, knowledge, and passion to navigate these challenges successfully. Your unique perspective as an entrepreneur brings a valuable voice to the business world, and your resilience can pave the way for future generations.

Stay strong, stay focused, and never lose sight of the incredible potential within you. You have what it takes to overcome any difficulty and thrive in your business. You've already overcome so much; you can do this too.

Who is she?

Internationally acclaimed and widely respected, Yushima Cherry Burks, LMSW, stands as a beacon of hope and transformation through her impactful work. As the published author of *Picking Up the Pieces to 100 Broken Promises* and the insightful *Companion Workbook to Picking Up the Pieces to 100 Broken Promises*, Yushima is the driving force behind Chatterbox Therapists, a subsidiary of Year of Yushima LLC.

With a profound dedication to individuals and families, Yushima approaches her role with utmost seriousness, recognizing that helping people navigate the complexities of life is a noble endeavour. Her career spans over two decades, focusing on families and survivors dealing with abuse and traumatic experiences. A pivotal achievement in her journey was the establishment of the nationally recognized program "JUST US," which held a central role within the YWCA for seven years.

Yushima's purpose crystallizes in her passion for helping survivors heal from the depths of abuse-induced trauma, while also fuelling the empowerment of others to recognize their intrinsic potential and worth. While renowned for her effervescent personality, Yushima is resolute when confronting injustices, advocating against abuse, and raising awareness on neglect. She embodies the roles of both a protective mama bear and a loving wife. Guided by a deep personal relationship with her faith, Yushima finds the motivation to persist in "the work" that she is dedicated to.

Moreover, Yushima Cherry Burks is an adept teacher, equipping individuals, families, and communities with the tools to reclaim joy and vitality amidst adversity. Her endeavours extend beyond the written word; a percentage from every purchase of her work contributes to aiding victims on their journey towards healing from the ravages of abuse.

Yushima Cherry Burks is the embodiment of resilience, and her contributions resonate across various platforms. She stands as the internationally known published author of not only her impactful books, but also journals and other enlightening works. With an unfaltering commitment to making a difference, Yushima's presence continues to inspire survivor healing and advocacy. Her legacy is a testament to the power of personal transformation, and she remains a force to be reckoned with both personally and professionally.

"Many of us have faced similar hurdles and uncertainties, and it is through the support of our village that we can overcome them."
- **Yushima Cherry Burks**

CHATTERBOX THERAPISTS

SUPPORTING YOUR WELL-BEING

SERVICES

- Self-Care for the Professional
- Couples Coupling
- Social Work Supervisor Training
- Mastering Marriage
- Support for Parents of Neurodivergent Children
- G.O.A.L.S. Masterclass
- The Co-Parenting Masterclass
- The Psychology of Parenting

📍 1430 Gadsden Highway, Ste 116-733, Birmingham, Alabama 35235, United States

📞 (256) 299-5877 🌐 www.chatterboxtherapists.com

Alecia Latoya Henry

Beauty in Entrepreneurship and Creativity

"Our mindset and circumstances influence our entrepreneurial journey. When we're pushed to our limits, we often discover untapped reservoirs of determination and creativity. In contrast, when comfort cushions our efforts, we might inadvertently hinder our business's potential."

Reflecting on my journey as an entrepreneur, I've come to realize that so many of the experiences I've undergone in the past have played a pivotal role in shaping who I am today. One of the things I've always known about myself is that I possess a natural inclination for leadership. This inherent quality has been evident throughout my life as I've found people looking to me for guidance and direction, whether it's in workplaces or other settings.

There's a particular moment that stands out in my memory as a turning point, signifying one of the many driving forces in my ability to take initiative. This moment occurred during my time working at a hotel. I distinctly remember a day when our boss was going around assigning tasks to everyone. As I observed this scene unfolding, I couldn't help but feel a sense of urgency about the situation. Without hesitation, I voiced my thoughts to my colleagues, expressing that the mindset of waiting for instructions was akin to a "slave mentality." I urged them to embrace proactivity and take the initiative to get things done instead of waiting to be asked by their superior.

When I spoke those words to my colleagues, I could sense their surprise and curiosity. What truly mattered to me, however, was that my message resonated with them. I could see it in the way they looked at me — as someone who was willing to challenge the norm and inspire a different way of thinking. My candid words had struck a chord, and it was evident that my perspective was shifting the dynamics in the room. I recognized my role as a leader who could guide, inspire, and drive change. It was during that moment that I fully embraced the notion that I was destined to be more than just a follower; I was meant to be a leader, a decision-maker, and ultimately, an entrepreneur.

Growing up, I was always fascinated by beauty. My mom used to say that "your hair is your beauty," and that resonated with me. I always wanted to go to the beauty salon with my older cousin and that's where my passion for beauty started.

As a teenager, I enjoyed doing my friends' and neighbours' hair, and as I got older, my love for beauty grew as did my passion. When I became an adult, and having worked in different fields, I knew for a fact that I wanted to own a website to sell hair and beauty products but had very little idea of how to go about it. Then, a few years ago, I travelled overseas and met a lady, who I connected with and we became "long distant" friends. One day, she called and introduced me to a business idea to which I listened attentively. I said yes to everything she said because she was giving me the opportunity to do exactly what I wanted. I felt like that was the moment when the pieces of my dream started to fall in place. It started to feel real, possible, and inevitable.

Before she hung up, she said, "I am going to help you start a business, and that is my Mother's Day gift to you." She suggested that I think about everything she said, and then make a final decision and let her know when I was ready. I didn't need long to think about it. I had always wanted to launch this business idea. When the website was bought and handed to me, I remember her saying something that changed everything about me. She said, "You are now a business owner." It stirred up something inside me — a feeling that I was longing to experience.

Even though I didn't have any knowledge about owning or running a website, what it entails, and how I was going to maintain it, I knew I was not going to turn down the opportunity.

So, my friend paid for the website to be created for me, and I was left to get the legal aspect of it completed, as I wanted my business to be registered as a legal business. The struggles that came with wanting to get the business legalized and off the ground were painful. Staying up for hours at nights customizing the website, adding products and researching to learn more about a new business, was very tedious and draining.

I gave up on this business 100 times. I went through so much trying to figure out how to operate this business. On numerous occasions, I would sit and cry. I didn't think I could do it. I remember telling myself that it's not even worth the energy and the effort, and that I just wanted to do away with it. I remember calling my friend and crying to her, telling her that I was going to let this business go. When she said, "Don't give up; it will work out," my hope was revived.

Added to the challenges of developing the website, I had to change the business name. I had to find one that was suitable for registration, which was kind of emotional, because I had a name that I wanted to use which was special to me.

With me still not having enough knowledge and still learning through the process, I had to figure out a domain name and how to obtain one. I was never spoon fed or had information presented to me. I had to research everything that I needed to know and I felt like it was taking too much out of me. However, there was always a voice in the back of my head — and a good friend in my ear — telling me to not give up.

Speaking about friends and support, I want to divert for a second to focus on mentors and role models. One person who has significantly impacted my journey is my dear friend, Nikisha Brown. Nikisha's story is truly inspiring. We've been friends since our early days in primary school, and what sets our friendship apart is the deep understanding we share. Our connection originates from knowing each other's backgrounds, experiences, and dreams. Notably, our friendship has never encountered any disagreements because we have an understanding that keeps us in harmony.

Nikisha's story is a testament to how resilient and determined one can be regardless of what they have been through. Growing up, she faced significant challenges, including her mother's inability to care for her due to other responsibilities. Despite these adversities, Nikisha never lost sight of her dreams. She pursued an education with fortitude, a determination that became even more evident as she navigated her journey while being pregnant and attending school simultaneously.

One of the most motivating aspects of Nikisha's journey is her commitment to her goals. She completed high school and then ventured into further education, earning degrees in both marketing and psychology. Her dedication didn't waver even when faced with the challenges of pregnancy and continuing her studies. Nikisha's story exemplifies the power of setting your mind to something and relentlessly pursuing it, which has had a profound impact on me. Her experiences and accomplishments resonate deeply, reminding me that circumstances need not define our destinies. Her example has ingrained in me the belief that I can overcome any obstacles and achieve my aspirations, regardless of my background or available resources. In pursuit of my business, I continuously draw on her story for inspiration when necessary.

To share Nikisha's message of empowerment with other women, I emphasize the lessons I've learned from her journey. No matter your starting point or the resources at your disposal, you have the potential to succeed if you remain determined and focused. Nikisha's journey instils the confidence to pursue our dreams persistently, even when the odds seem stacked against us. Her story is a living proof that where there's a will, there's a way — a mantra that I hold dear in my pursuit of entrepreneurial success.

Nevertheless, becoming an entrepreneur has opened my eyes to the myths and misconceptions that often surround business. One such myth is the notion that starting a business is as simple as waking up one day, creating a website, stocking up on products, and voila, success and riches will follow. This couldn't be further from the truth. The reality is that entrepreneurship is far from easy. It's a journey that demands careful planning, meticulous research, and dedication.

The heart of the matter is that the road to success in business is paved with challenges and complexities. It's not just about having a product or service to offer, it's also about distinguishing oneself in a crowded marketplace. With countless competitors vying for attention, the crucial question is, what sets you apart? Why should someone choose to support your business amidst a sea of options?

Moreover, the ebb and flow of business must also be acknowledged. There are seasons when profits surge, and others when they dip. Planning ahead, managing finances, and preparing for both scenarios is a fundamental aspect of entrepreneurship.

While reflecting on these intricacies, I've had to look at the role I play in hindering the success of my business; one of the challenges that I continue to face on this journey. Yes, the business is doing okay, but it could do extremely well if I were to change my approach for example. Instead of committing 20 hours to my business in the week, I could commit 40; however, I choose to work those 40 hours building someone else's dream in their company. I've pondered how different my approach might be if my livelihood depended solely on the business. It's natural to contemplate the impact of such a scenario. Perhaps I would be more driven to secure the resources needed, even in the face of adversity. It's essential to recognize these thoughts and motivations, as they shape our commitment and undertakings.

At times, comfort can be a silent deterrent. Having a fallback option, such as a stable job, can inadvertently lull us into complacency. We might find ourselves content with the business's performance in a given month, especially when external factors are providing some stability. Yet, true success requires continuous dedication and effort. A business left to its own devices, without proactive attention, can quickly become stagnant.

This introspection has led me to contemplate how our mindset and circumstances influence our entrepreneurial journey. When we're pushed to our limits, we often discover untapped reservoirs of determination and creativity. In contrast, when comfort cushions our efforts, we might inadvertently hinder our business's potential.

Though I wish I could dedicate more time to my business, I continue to choose to not give up for many reasons. One of the main reasons why I never give up is because the business was a gift to me from someone who met me once and hardly even know me, yet believed in me; I never want to disappoint her. My only choice is to believe in myself as much as she does. All the work that was put in, I could not just watch it go in vain. I want to see it come to fruition.

Another reason was that I have always wanted to be a business owner because of the freedom that comes with it. I've never wanted to report to anyone but me. I've always wanted to just have the freedom and peace of mind that there is no one above me and that I was my own boss. That desire makes me push harder.

I also wanted another source of income and I saw where this business could potentially become a great source of one — if done right.

I have given up easily in the past on things that never showed any sign of working out, and I felt like I owed this to myself, to prove to myself that I can do it.

I envisioned lying in bed on mornings when I don't feel like working and getting up when I am mentally and physically prepared. It felt like everything that I envisioned was possible through this business and that its success held the key to what I imagined.

I could see where this business would be the stepping stone and the starting point of something new, so it made and continues to make me push harder even through the tears, sweat, and sleepless nights.

Overcoming the odds of not giving up is very hard, but personal at the same time. It takes knowing what you want and being intentional about it. Having a dream and a goal of what the end result looks like.

Life is not easy and nothing comes easy. Working for yourself is harder than working for someone else. You have to make it work. Your survival depends on how much work you put in. What you put in is what you will get out. You put in nothing; you get nothing.

Now, let me leave you with a few things as you progress on your journey of entrepreneurship. First, ask yourself, "If I give up, who is going to do it for me?" That question should trigger the sensation of persistence.

Finally, I will leave you with two quotes:

1. "The difference between a successful person and others is not a lack of strength, not a lack of knowledge, but rather a lack of persistence." - Vince Lombardi

2. "Change happens when the pain of staying the same becomes greater than the pain of making a change." - Tony Robbins

Who is she?

Originally from the vibrant landscapes of Jamaica, Alecia Henry is an inspiring entrepreneur. With a resolute spirit and an innate ability to find beauty in every facet of life, Alecia's journey has been marked by self-motivation and a profound sense of purpose.

At a remarkably young age, Alecia's fascination with the world of beauty and entrepreneurship ignited a spark that would later illuminate her path. In the world of business, she stands as a testament to the power of dreams, having successfully established her own business that reflects her dedication.

Alecia's passion for beauty transcends mere aesthetics. To her, beauty resonates from within, radiating outward to illuminate the world. This belief has not only guided her personal ethos but has also sculpted the foundation of her entrepreneurial journey.

A voracious reader, Alecia's insatiability for knowledge is unparalleled. Challenges become stepping stones in her relentless pursuit of growth and insight. She recognizes that in today's digital age, information is a boundless resource, empowering her to explore any subject that piques her curiosity and continue to develop her skills and knowledge to be able to serve her business.

Central to her philosophy is the conviction that a mere thought, once nurtured and fortified with self-affirmation, has the potential to reshape destinies. She firmly subscribes to the notion that the universe aligns itself with those who wholeheartedly believe in the manifestation of their aspirations.

Alecia's journey serves as an embodiment of determination, creativity, and the limitless potential of the human spirit. Through her ventures, she not only shapes her own narrative but also empowers others to harness their inner brilliance. With every endeavour she undertakes, she reinforces the idea that true beauty emerges when authenticity and purpose converge.

As a Jamaican content creator, Alecia's creative expression resonates deeply with her roots. She encapsulates the vibrant spirit of her homeland, infusing her work with a unique blend of culture and individuality. Through her content, she not only reflects her own journey but also inspires and empowers others to embrace their own paths.

Alecia Henry stands as a luminous example of how youthful determination, boundless creativity, and an unbreakable spirit can pave the way for remarkable achievements. Her journey showcases that beauty is not merely skin deep, but an essence that permeates every facet of life. As she continues to evolve and create, Alecia radiates the transformative power of embracing one's inner beauty and using it to illuminate the world through entrepreneurship and creativity.

"No matter your starting point or the resources at your disposal, you have the potential to succeed if you remain determined and focused."
- **Alecia Henry**

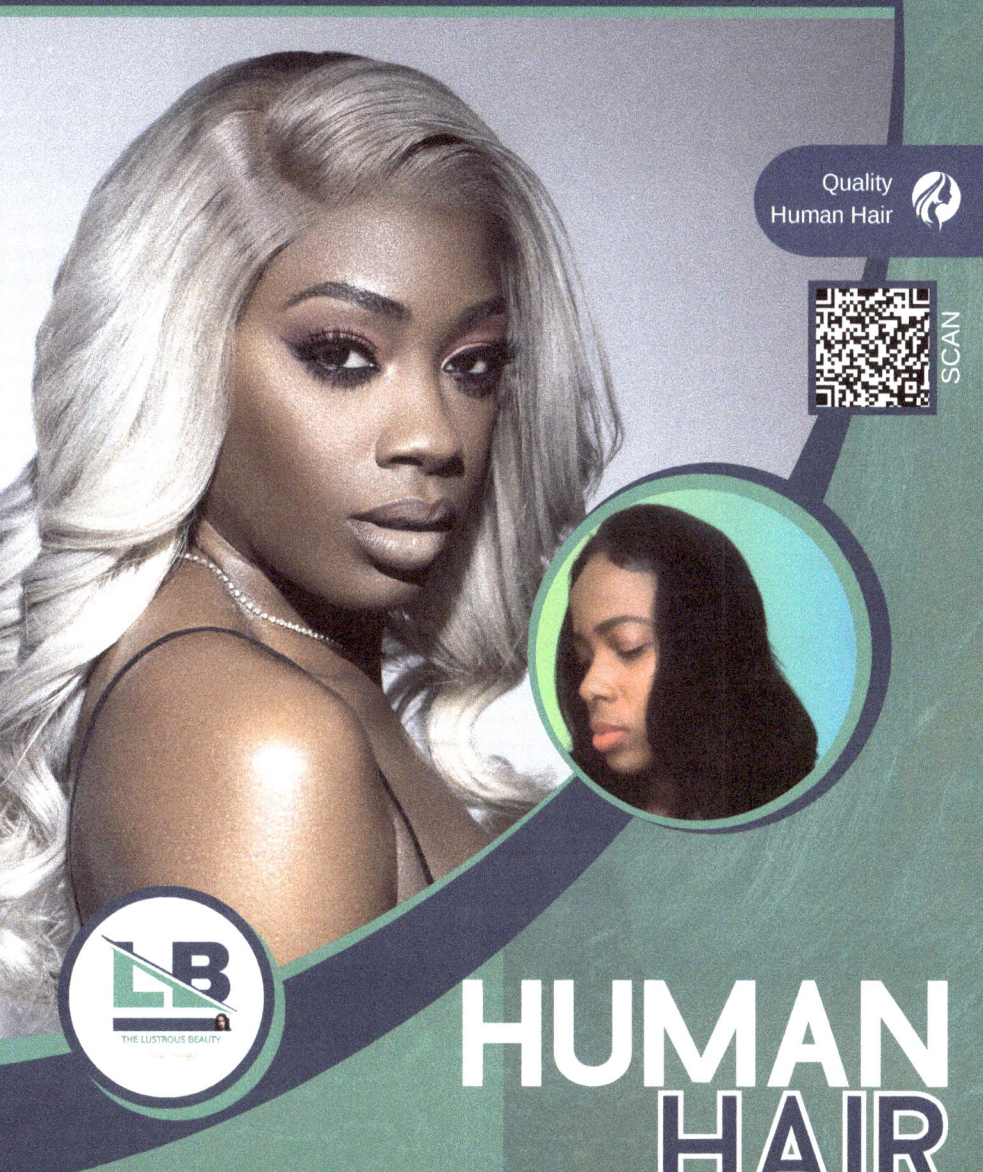

Janair Johnson

Resilience in Every Step

"As a Black woman, any woman, or any person wanting to start something of your own and get into entrepreneurship, go for it. You will never know the exact way that the wheels will turn, but you have to get started."

Life in the shoes of a female entrepreneur can be an interesting journey. Regardless of whether your walk into success was by choice or you stumbled into it by a divine sequence of events, it's going to change your life. It will require you to be fearless. Discipline will be your best friend as you build the life you are destined to achieve. You are in the driver's seat, so show up for yourself. You'll have to sit out on some events with friends and miss so much more, but it will all be worth it.

I've always known that I was destined to own multiple businesses because my mind has always been a creative one. The pool to use all of my talents made it hard to narrow it down to just one gift; I saw how they could all be intertwined beautifully. After all, God didn't give them to me just so I could set them idly by the wayside. Music, cooking, hair, making products, public speaking, coaching and advising, image consulting; they are all connected in some way. They all represent beauty to me. To use all of my talents, I have moved from state to state, received training and learned so many beauty industry secrets, and have always been excited for everything new I was experiencing. Consistently defining my craft makes me feel invincible.

Young and ambitious, I wanted it all. However, as a wife and mother, I realized quickly that it wasn't going to be as smooth as I thought it would be. Still, I knew it was not impossible. You hear all the stories about entrepreneurship and how it is a wonderful life of freedom, and it is, but you definitely will put in the work for it. I've had many long, anxiety filled nights. I've had days when I've cried, feeling like there was no one who understands me because I didn't have any other entrepreneurs around me. Wanting to be in a better space of likeminded people, I began to search for a new community. I began working with other independents in my profession and we began forming small groups. We would all get together and attend hair and beauty professional shows. Though, it was very refreshing to talk the cosmos/beauty language, meet new people, and not be in competition with them, there was still a gap to be filled. I knew nothing about business and had to learn along the way.

Now, let me take you back to where it all began to give you a better understanding. I have always been creative and knew that I wanted to be in business, but I didn't really know much about the right protocols and how-tos of being in business officially. What I did have in abundance, though, was the taste and hunger for success. I got married at the age of 20, and by 21, I had my first child. I started my small business, Janair's Mobile Styles, before my son was born, and when he was, I still had to work. I had a small salon at home. However, as a mobile business, I had to travel all around town with my baby boy in tow — car seat, stroller, baby bag, hair caboodle; check! I would make my rounds to my clients' homes or their businesses to perform services for them and I had to be a mom while doing it. I'd have to nurse my son between services and even sometimes take breaks during the service to attend to him. I had to be a mom but I was dedicated and determined to make my business a success. My son was mild mannered and well behaved, so I wasn't frowned upon. Now, let me not forget, he was "oh so cute!" Everyone loved him; he was the nephew.

As the business grew and the momentum of success compounded, I decided to take a risky business move. I made the decision to go into business with a *dear* loved one: Worst decision that I ever made. Talk about a total scam. This really took me for a loop and left me in complete disbelief. This was one of the first instances when I wanted to give up on entrepreneurship. We'd always been close. I thought that this could be a next level opportunity for the business. We would walk and discuss all the possibilities and what it would look like being in business together. Well, after many walks and discussions, I moved forward without a contract. I went into business with this dear loved one and we built out a small, intimate, three persons salon. A salon that I never worked in at all.

When we built out the salon, I was so proud of us. I had put all of my hard earned money into this project. I didn't even have a credit card at the time, so everything was cash or check. I had become a single mom by now — that's another story for another time — and was also working for a hotel at the time. Additionally, I was also a student, studying business management. Yes, on top of all this, I was being a dedicated mom, spending every moment I could with my son and still taking him with me to work. My son went to school with me too. He had become my partner in business. He was my inspiration and I knew I couldn't let him down.

Unfortunately, I never completed my schooling. I have dyslexia, which makes learning written work very challenging. Nevertheless, I've learned how to teach myself things easier over the years.

The opportunity to open my first brick and mortar shop with a loved one seemed like a perfect idea, but hindsight is 20/20. Anyway, as we got closer to opening day, I noticed some changes in my loved one's behaviour. There was suddenly a lack of communication; I wasn't sure why until I received an invitation to be a guest at the grand opening of *our* business. Of course, this threw me off. I was under the impression that it was 'our business,' so why would I need an invitation to my own grand opening, right?

This dear loved one informed me that we were not in business together and this was their business. Going on to say that they knew that I would have the ability to obtain the money to assist in the build out of the shop and help with the overseeing of the entire project, so they thought the decision to bring me on board was the best idea. They went on to further insult me by saying they figured I could work for them. I was so taken aback. What could I do, though? I had no paperwork. This is family and someone I trusted, so I didn't think I would need any. I could've tried to get all the money that I spent back for the project but how was I going to fight it with no agreement in place? So, I decided to learn the valuable lesson and move on: You can't trust people sometimes and that's really sad to say.

Not long after that deflating experience, I moved to a new state. I was off to begin a new independent journey. I was starting from the bottom. I arrived in Arizona with two suitcases, two people — I was pregnant — and $2000 to my name. God only knows the grace He's shown me and the favour He's placed in my life. I wasn't sure how I was going to navigate my new home. It was difficult to provide for my children. I wasn't getting child support or any government assistance. I didn't have the proper income either; I was making $8.40 an hour. I needed some sort of income, so while I worked on building a clientele in this new state, I had to take a job at a salon and that's what they paid — totalling about $19,000 a year. Insane. Nonetheless, I did my best to provide an awesome lifestyle with what I had and make everything feel like quality, strategizing how I could take advantage of any discounts and savings.

Do you know the saying, "How to make a dollar out of fifteen cents?" Well, here's an idea of what that looks like. I couldn't even afford to have a meal out once a week. McDonald's had the $0.99 meal menu and even that was a push because I was so insufficiently funded. I couldn't afford to spend more than $3 at McDonald's per week, so I would go there after my work shift on Thursdays and pick up a double cheeseburger and French fries from the dollar menu and ask for an extra bun. I would then walk almost a mile to the bus stop to get home and share one special meal with my son; kids LOVE McDonald's.

I was new to the area and a single mom of two now and the pressure to have peace and fiscally support my family was on more than ever. The territory was not very cultured but it was promising. This was a bonus for me. It gave me an advantage because that meant there weren't many Black owned salons in the area. Eventually, I was able to find a suite that was just right, in the heart of Scottsdale where I was living. Things were coming together slowly. I was filled with excitement to service my community. The salon wasn't going to magically fill up, so I had to hustle. Back then, we had the Yellow Pages — the phonebook — so I got on my phone and started calling all the local businesses that seemed like they could use image consulting services or just partner with companies for employee discounts with my salon.

One day, while networking, I met a man by the name of Mr. Joe, who was the owner of a business having adult parties for a high profile, exclusive clientele. I didn't even really know what that meant. However, I soon learned that it was just a big swingers orgy fest. He was in the adult entertainment industry with his wife who was a porn star. I was a bit naïve. I didn't really understand all the details of what adult parties looked like. He made it sound so cool and chilled.

We started meeting for business meetings at the salon where I worked, working out the details on how our business could pair together. He also told me that he was a licensed computer tech and built computers. Honestly, again, I was so naïve back then, I never noticed that anytime I suggested that we meet at his office there was always something going on. Long story short, he and I did sign a contract; only, he never gave me my copy. He said he would email it to me and never did.

He took my computer to fix the charger port as well as do any necessary windows updates that I needed. I'm not the biggest tech person, so I went along and believed that he was skilful and knowledgeable enough to help. After all, he was my new found friend, a Black man, and as I stated before, there were very few of us, so I didn't know I had a reason to not trust him. Finally, the day came where we were to have this huge event, but little did I know, he had a trick up his sleeve.

This was a crucial moment for me as my business was brand new and I was counting on every single dollar that I needed to make on the night. I expected to make $500 for a few hours and get home just after midnight as it was New Year's Eve. When I arrived at the event, he told me that the marketing for my services had not gone down so well because he never sent out the flyers and emails that I would be available. He didn't let people know that they could register for my beauty services. They had no idea that I would be available if they needed a blowout, lashes or quick makeup, manicure/polish change, nothing. He then asked me if I would be comfortable working the door. That was not the plan, but he would pay me the same. Fine, how hard could that be?

People started to check in; the line was building up quickly. It was practically out the door. I remember thinking, *If this is so exclusive, how does so many people know about it?* There were people who weren't on the list and not the calibre he explained would attend, but he said to let them in and so, I did. Well, this posed another problem. Instead of just checking people in, those who had already paid, and giving them wristbands, I now had to sell new entries to the event. This meant that I had to process payments. Believe it or not, this established business did not have a credit card processor, so I had to use my business' Square account to process payments for them. I was trying to be a team player and show that I was very supportive. I wanted them to see that I was an asset to the team. I definitely wanted to be a recommended source for other businesses in the area.

When I was finished processing all the payments, I gave them the cash for every processed credit card attendee that used my service system. What a mistake of the day! When it was all over, not a single person attached to this event received payment for their services. These people stiffed the hotel, me, the equipment crew, and other contracted workers. It was terrible. Then they went missing. When the dust slightly cleared, I started to go over conversations we'd had. I remembered him telling me that they changed their company's locations often because their parties had been shut down for getting too rowdy. I realised that there were so many red flags that I hadn't paid attention to. Not only was I out of the money he was supposed to pay me, but I was also out of my own money and the time it took me to prepare for the event; I had given him all the money in cash from people who swiped credit cards to my account and it was on New Year's, so I missed my son's second New Year's. I was also out of a computer as I never got it back. In all honesty, I wasn't set up to take a hit like that by any means.

I was already getting extensions to pay my rent and car note. Each month, after paying bills, I would have like $23 left over, sometimes even less. This was a very hard hit but I knew I could not live like that, so I just had to brush it off and keep grinding. There was no time to just sit and dwell on it. I had to keep moving. I had to be an overcomer and diva was the new female hustle.

Back to the Yellow Pages and grinding it out in the salon I went. Things eventually picked up and I remained in this location for approximately seven years. Then, one day, this enchanting thing happened. I came across a beautiful salon space that was so perfect. I called the realtor, met up with them two days later, and moved in seven days later. It was perfect. My second shot at a brick and mortar store for myself! This time, I was way more prepared. I had several extension and wig lines by that time, which all went by collection; there was the Every Day Girl, Good Girl, Premium, Elite line, and last but not least, the synthetic hair blends. It was so exciting to decorate, clean, and get the salon together, preparing for my grand opening.

Who would've seen this coming, though? We got the announcement for Covid. *What is Covid?* I thought. Whatever it was, it sounded crazy, and honestly, most of us were in disbelief. My soft opening/grand opening was scheduled for March 13, 2020, which is officially Glitter N Bliss day in my city. On March 11, a national announcement was made, suggesting that people stay indoors. People were advised to not go to gatherings as they were going to start shutting down the towns. *What? Wait a minute. This cannot be happening! How long is this going to last?* I didn't know what I was going to do. The lockdown happened and it was a tough time. I couldn't open the salon, so there would be no income from that and I didn't know how long that would last. Luckily, I was no stranger to hard times, so I squared up with it.

I got creative. I started making products. Everyone had always been asking me about products to use on Black hair, so I figured; hey, we're at home, so why not? I came out with over 17 products during the lockdown! There's almost always a rainbow at the end of every storm, and this proved that. This was a big key to my survival and success. I was able to make sales and I didn't have to lose revenue. Covid brought something out of me that I wasn't even sure that I could do. I never ever thought that I could actually have my own products, make commercials, or start a nonprofit. So many wonderful things came out of Covid.

What I want you to learn from my struggles as an entrepreneur is that there is always an upside after you fall. Every time you fall, just know that you're in a learning moment and when you stand up, you can begin to use that lesson. Even if you're having to learn the same lesson multiple times, every experience is a little different.

So, I will leave you with this: As a Black woman, any woman, or any person wanting to start something of your own and get into entrepreneurship, go for it. You will never know the exact way that the wheels will turn, but you have to get started. Once the wheels start turning, there will begin to be a flow, and the support will come. The ideas will too, and so will the funding if you have something special that the world needs. You're the only one who can give and bring that thing that only you can do to the market.

Virtual high-fives to everyone who will catapult into the next chapter of their life and push through barriers and obstacles that try to make one succumb to quitting. I dare you to keep believing, keep dreaming, and continue putting one foot in front of the other.

My mom always says, "As sure as night falls, the sun will rise in the morning."

Who is she?

Janair Johnson is an accomplished stylist and visionary entrepreneur, proudly serving as the driving force behind Glitter and Bliss Salon, a premier establishment nestled in the vibrant heart of Scottsdale, Arizona. Originally from the vibrant city of Chicago, Janair has curated a remarkable journey spanning over fifteen years within the dynamic world of hairstyling and beauty. Her journey, marked by dedication and a deep passion for her craft, has led her to thrive in some of the most fiercely competitive markets, from the sun-soaked landscapes of Southern California to the cultural epicentre of Atlanta, Ohio.

Janair is a living embodiment of continuous growth and development, a lifelong learner with an insatiable thirst for mastering her craft. She has conscientiously sought out and completed a range of courses led by luminaries within the beauty industry, immersing herself in cutting-edge techniques and innovative methodologies. This commitment to excellence is a cornerstone of her identity, ensuring that her clients receive nothing short of the highest quality services.

As a stylist, Janair's skills encompass a vast spectrum, reflecting her profound expertise across various hair types. Her signature lies in her remarkable ability to create and maintain healthy hair, transcending mere aesthetics to focus on the overall well-being of her clients. Her prowess extends across key domains:

- **Weave and Extension Techniques**: Janair has honed her proficiency in weaving and extension techniques, seamlessly blending artistry with precision to deliver transformative results.
- **Hair Colouring**: A true virtuoso, she has an innate knack for bringing life and vibrancy to hair through her impeccable colouring techniques.
- **Aesthetics**: Beyond hair, Janair has an uncanny ability to curate aesthetics that empower and inspire. Her work transcends the ordinary, crafting visual narratives that captivate.
- **Lashes and Brows**: With an artist's touch, she crafts luscious lashes and perfectly sculpted brows, accentuating the beauty in every face she touches.

- **Professional Makeup for Publication**: Janair's talents extend to makeup artistry, a skill she wields to elevate clients for both the camera and real life.

In addition to her remarkable skills as a stylist, Janair is a dedicated educator, sharing her wisdom and expertise with fellow stylists, aspiring professionals, and even at fashion and hair shows. Her ability to convey her knowledge and insights has made her a sought-after presence in the industry.

Janair's clientele isn't confined to individuals seeking personal transformations; her work extends to collaborations with photographers, gracing the pages of esteemed local and regional publications.

Beyond her remarkable professional achievements, Janair has a philanthropic heart, actively giving back to her community through volunteering with Freshstart for Women, a testament to her desire to uplift and empower those around her.

With her finger on the pulse of evolving trends and an unyielding commitment to her craft, Janair Johnson continues to shape the beauty landscape and inspire countless individuals to embrace their own unique allure.

For inquiries and collaborations, reach out to Janair at janairj@glitternbliss.com.

"You'll have to sit out on some events with friends and miss so much more, but it will all be worth it."
- **Janair Johnson**

Glitter n Bliss

GNB & RIANAJ by Janair Johnson

Your one stop shop for High Quality...

- Hair Weaves
- Hair Extensions
- Human Hair Wigs
- Hair Colors & Highlights

in Scottsdale, Phoenix, AZ and the Surrounding Area

Get the look...

It's simpler than you think.

 www.glitternbliss.com 📞 602-427-7063

Dudu Mathebula

Be Ready to Adapt to Change

"As an entrepreneur, you cannot be rigid and not want to change. With each curveball you experience along the way, your adaptability will fuel your creativity and help you to remain relevant."

My name is Dudu Mathebula. I am a unique, aspirant young woman who's determined to succeed in all that I do, whether it be parenting, romance, or in health and fitness. I have this intense pensive look when I am not smiling, which resembles how much of a deep thinker and analytical person I am. That face works for me in boardrooms, I guess, but in my private life, everyone knows me as a sweet, opinionated, kind, and gentle soul.

Professionally, I recently completed a course in digital marketing at the University of Cape Town. Many years ago, I studied photojournalism at the renowned institute, The Market Photo Workshop. In 2007, I started my career as a media manager in newspaper print, and this career spanned over 11 years in digital and television broadcasting.

It was loads of fun for many years and paid well; media practitioners in South Africa were unstoppable, and breaking news, compelling headlines, tight deadlines, and multiple angles to cover stories were endless, given the rich history of our country and its young democracy. It was fun… Until it wasn't. The tides changed, and traditional media was replaced by citizen journalism; print copies were already old news because of the rise of the digital age. Things were changing fast, and everything we knew about media was slowly unravelling around us; it was time for a change.

I left print media with a pocket of money and an aspirant heart to start my first-ever business. It was a multimedia business, and it was called See Mo Media. I joined forces with a friend and colleague, and we planned to get into the creative arts. We started well and got ourselves an office in the hustle and bustle of a new hub for business in Maboneng, Johannesburg. We built solid connections along the way. We did studio photography, styled our own sets, and shot music videos for up-and-coming musicians, as well as prominent musicians such as Slikour and DJ Glen Lewis. We were sought after by choreographers and artists in the entertainment business, and had a positive first year in business.

After the paraphernalia and hype died down, we soon realized that we were going broke, our business was not sustainable, and our production work was only as good as a TikTok trend. After a little while, people were over our content, and they moved on to other creative work because the sea of visual creativity is vast. We had to let go of our office and cut down on our production teams to the point where it was just the two of us again, all alone, without money, and with our tails between our legs. We had to return to work and find media jobs to make ends meet.

The curtailing of our beloved business not only felt like a catastrophic failure but also put us into bankruptcy. We were utterly devastated. The process taught me many things about business and the time and effort required to run a business. In hindsight, we knew very little about business, and we were ill-prepared, naive, and immature youngsters with very little knowledge about business investment and how to acquire it. It was a learning curve, an experience I do not regret. Had it not been for it, I would not be in business today.

A single mom raised me, and my father passed on when I was 16 years old, as I was nearing the end of high school. My mother firmly believes in women making their own money and has always started micro businesses. She dabbled in catering and transport services, and at some point, she was running her hair salon in the 90s from our car garage at home. I suppose that's where my desire for business emanated from.

At the start of the COVID-19 pandemic, my business partner, Dikeledi (Deekay), and I started a three-year-old branding enterprise called Colour Central. We started it with zero capital, no inventory, and no overheads; we still don't yet have physical premises. At one point, we had an online store that we were hosting with Shopify. It was a great tool, considering the kind of climate when we launched it; people were mainly buying online and had a lot of disposable income due to working from home and rarely going out. As the pandemic conditions improved, restrictions were eased, and the demand for our content also experienced all-time lows. Eventually, we decided to close the online store.

At the inception of Colour Central, our cash cow became our queer clothing and accessories ranges, and it soon became our corporate identity faster than we could realize. We faced the reality that it was impossible to be a new business without a focal point; we could not present Colour Central as a jack-of-all-trades firm, we had to focus on one idea at a time, and so we continued into markets, selling our Pride merchandise. We soon realized that this linear focus wasn't generating enough revenue to sustain the business. We were focused on obtaining just queer business. In essence, most of our business came from the community in the form of individual purchases and queer, human rights focused organisations.

In our third year in business, we decided to reposition our service offering. We started branching out and approached multi-faceted industries such as television broadcasting, where we were supplying and branding office stationery, pens, and bags for conferences. We grew into making crew garments, working with big-name production houses such as Burnt Onion, Seriti, and Netflix, who produce TV shows such as Redemption. We did similar work for an engineering and cleaning company, and have continued to spread our wings with these small to medium enterprises.

One of the key takeaways that we have learned along the way is that your initial business idea will evolve over time. As an entrepreneur, you cannot be rigid and not want to change. With each curveball you experience along the way, your adaptability will fuel your creativity and help you to remain relevant. Our initial idea was to buy an ice-cream and milkshake machine which costs half a million rands. Yes, we saw the potential of revenue from it; however, it did not mean that we were passionate about dessert. On the contrary, the irony is that my business partner and I are into fitness, wellness, and healthy eating. What remained was that we both had a desire to be in business. Thus, the ideation process and allowing the evolution of these ideas led us to coming back to ourselves, to who we are, our passions, and values.

We didn't believe we were deviating from our original plan; we were seeking alternative routes in order to reach our goals. We weren't frustrated by not having capital to start to the point where we gave up on business altogether. We eventually arrived at a place where we could discover meaning in the work that we were doing. The constant affirmations along the way were also positive signs that we were becoming more aligned with who we are.

Deekay's passion for advocacy and activism shows in the way that people appreciate our visibility at markets and advocating for young people who feel marginalised by their communities. Our presence makes them feel important, appreciated, and seen. Our pride stalls have created an impact such that our patrons relay their stories of coming out to their families. One lady from Uganda became so emotional and appreciated that, in South Africa, we are free to sell and wear gay colours with pride, which is not the case in the country she originates from. My passion for branding communication has also evolved in such a way that I am able to design and package solutions for corporations, still fulfilling my love for giving brands a voice and help position their brands.

Ultimately, we both trusted the process, and I believe we are right where we are meant to be. Entrepreneurship is a long road with bends and up and down hills, and the lesson is that each experience has given us a spirit of humility. Many doors will be shut but many more will open just as long as you stay the course, remain teachable, learning and growing from your mistakes.

I have personally found that some processes in business can be very complex, and if you don't persist to get over the knowledge hurdle, you stop growing. A practical example is accounting for business. If you don't have a natural flair for numbers, it will be an uphill to learn. In business, numbers are the very breath of a business, even if you choose to outsource the service, you will still need to know the basics of complying with what's required for tax obligations, etc. There are tons of online resources out there that will teach you the ins and outs of business without breaking the bank. It's just about taking time to choose what's best for your business.

Business requires that you do what you love, "so that you will never work a day in your life;" I think that's how the saying goes. Discovering your passion and pursuing in business will help you enjoy the journey far more than selling ice cream.

We are currently working on establishing our printing hub and getting prime space where we can run our business from. With this revenue, we will launch the first ever pride store in our city. We are firm believers that it is impossible to serve two masters at the same time. Business requires your full attention, which is one of the biggest lessons that we have learned from our experience. Having a nine to five job has prevented us from growing and steering the business in the direction where it can reach its full potential. We are working on our exit strategies so that we can both grow Colour Central and take it to new heights.

We can make our digital catalogue available for possible partnerships with other entrepreneurs and organisations that would like to explore ways in which we can enlarge our footprint. We are still limited by international shipping for our custom-made pride garments but working out a cost effective plan around it.

Who is she?

Dudu Mathebula is a dynamic and aspirant young woman whose journey has been defined by creativity, continuous learning, and drive for success. Dudu's story is an inspiring testament to her evolution from a seasoned media manager to a thriving entrepreneur in the multimedia space.

Dudu's commitment to growth and learning led her to complete a course in digital marketing at the esteemed University of Cape Town. Her thirst for knowledge also led her to the doors of The Market Photo Workshop, a renowned institute, where she honed her skills in photojournalism. With a strong foundation in media, Dudu embarked on an 11-year journey as a media manager in newspaper print, immersing herself in the world of journalism and content creation.

It was her courageous step away from print media, however, that marked a significant turning point in Dudu's path. Venturing into entrepreneurship, she co-founded her first business, See Mo Media. This multimedia venture not only showcased her creativity but also provided invaluable lessons about the complexities of running a business. This experience, though challenging, armed her with invaluable skills and insights that would prove instrumental in her current business.

Dudu harnessed the lessons from her past to give life to her new venture, Colour Central. In her role as founder and partner, she spearheads a thriving business that has produced crew garments for prominent productions like Seriti, Burnt Onion, and even collaborated with industry giants like Netflix on TV shows such as Redemption. Beyond the world of entertainment, Colour Central also caters to local customers and clients abroad, crafting high-quality stationary that marries style and functionality.

"Many doors will be shut but many more will open just as long as you stay the course, remain teachable, learning and growing from your mistakes."
- **Dudu Mathebula**

LGBTQ+

Our brand was built on **creativity and innovation.**

CORPORATE PRODUCTS

We craft our clothing with **love and passion.**

An exciting personal and corporate branding business which focuses on servicing LGBTQ+ persons, organisations, and businesses. Our selection of merchandise is of good quality with the heart of the client at the top of our mind.

Colour Central

CONTACT US

+27 83 360 6082 / +27 81 774 5671
info@colourcentral.co.za
www.colourcentral.co.za

PARTNERSHIPS

Our branding solutions look after you and your organisation's needs, not just looking the part, but by consistent branding through all seasons. We have summer t-shirts, caps and hats, golf shirts, and winter hoodies, body warmers, sweatpants, construction outfits and more!

We partner with artists and thought leaders to advance worthwhile causes.

featured in **media.**

From branded stickers and take away gifts to event banners and more...

EVENT BRANDING

SCAN

We look forward to working with you; **thank you!**

Loreen Aisha Ochefu-Ogiri

Just Move

"Waiting for the 'perfect' conditions only stifles advancement. Whether it is selling beans or rice, the starting point is crucial. The size or scale doesn't matter; the act of beginning does."

Things seem to have always been difficult for me, both in my personal and business life. You see, my personal life resembles a battlefield at times, with its own wars and trials, but they eventually fade away or work themselves out. Growing up was quite a challenge, almost like navigating through constant conflict zones. Despite the challenges I faced in childhood, I managed to stay strong and mature quickly. I was raised by my mother and stepfather, although it felt more like being raised by a single mom. My stepfather was there, yet not really present; he wasn't particularly kind, so it was a struggle. My mom is hearing impaired and so is my stepdad. Consequently, I had to mature faster than my years, becoming their ears, always on high alert. I was attuned to their needs, as if I were hearing for two extra people.

Sometimes, when thoughts of my biological dad would arise, a tinge of sadness would wash over me. Particularly when I was unfairly blamed for incidents at home, or when I was not believed. My upbringing was a true challenge. Despite the love and effort my mom poured into me, and even though I attended a good private school, inside our home, chaos reigned. The image people saw externally — that of a cherished only child — starkly contrasted with the reality of the tumultuous home environment. Later in life, I decided to get married, an entirely new journey filled with its own set of difficulties.

These hurdles, in fact, played a significant role in the timing of my business launch. It both deterred me from starting earlier and, paradoxically, pushed me into my crafting business.

Reflecting back, I was always a creative child, skilled in various crafts. My friends recognized my artistic prowess; whether it was drawing, painting, or tackling any creative task they threw at me. However, I never saw these talents as potential sources of income or as the foundation for a business. My aspirations had always leaned towards becoming an accountant, and I clung to that goal. It wasn't until during my marriage, when I was faced with an array of challenges, that I found myself at home as a stay-at-home mom for nearly three years.

The turbulence of family dynamics hit me hard. Financially, I was virtually destitute. Not a single naira bore my name, neither in my bank account nor in my possession. Events like baby showers and birthday parties became intimidating spectacles for me, prompting me to remain indoors. I believed that outsiders were oblivious to my struggles and attending such events would only magnify my shortcomings. My isolation bred depression, anger, and frustration, emotions I was determined not to impart on my children but ones that affected them, nonetheless.

In the midst of this emotional turmoil, my mother visited one day. She mentioned that a cousin had recently given birth. The natural question of what gift to get for the baby arose. I hesitated, unsure of my options given my dire financial state. As I sifted through my old phone, I stumbled upon a YouTube video — a spark from my past. Memories of my childhood crochet skills flooded back. With just 600 naira, I ventured to the market and invested in crochet supplies. Thus began my journey of crafting various exquisite pieces for the newborn. Packed thoughtfully, these creations were sent with my mother.

Little did I know, this simple gesture marked the start of something bigger. The references and inquiries began to trickle in, fuelled by the artistic touch I had imparted to those crocheted gifts. Looking back, I realize that the challenges I overcame in my marriage had a profound influence on my business trajectory. As I navigated through personal struggles, they intertwined with the emergence of my craft business.

Enduring almost three years of depression was the price I had to pay for transforming my marriage into a stepping stone for my business. Having been on my own and being independent for so many years, I had to learn to exist in the institution of marriage. I was in a dark place, utterly consumed by despair.

Unexpectedly, something shifted. I started my business venture, and initially, it seemed to progress smoothly. I was doing something that I love and making a living from it. Things were going well, then, like a sudden plunge, it all went down a steep slope. Everything changed. A new challenge arose in my personal life, sending my business spiralling southwards. Despite the setback, I refused to surrender. The business had offered more promise than remaining confined at home, the pervasive feeling of insignificance amplifying each passing day. I had lost that business but I didn't want to give up. I wanted to give entrepreneurship another go. I decided to start another business. This wasn't an easy task. I had no support. Many looked at me and said, "You've started a business and failed, why do you want to start another one?"

In Nigeria, it's common for the community to discourage starting a new business. The cycle usually goes: start, stop, start again, then abandon, and because of this, people have little faith in one's business dreams. Amidst this, a new business idea sprouted, one that I knew I could do well: a makeup line. I launched it, selling makeup products to students and a wide range of individuals, extending even to distant customers. However, despite initial success, financial mismanagement led to bankruptcy. The profits disappeared into the many demands on the home front, and I was left with another failed business venture.

Depression's grip tightened, and I found myself in a place of immense sorrow. I cried; my anguish palpable. Nevertheless, a tiny seed of hope arose as I secured a job at a bank. For almost two years, I held this position, but it didn't align with my aspirations. It felt like I was merely biding my time, waiting for an opportunity to transition into something more aligned with my passions. During this period, I started importing shoes and bags from China, selling them to colleagues and expanding my clientele. Slowly, this business began to flourish, transcending the boundaries of my workplace to reach a broader audience.

This success enabled me to leave the bank, and I was making substantial income from the business. However, upon deciding to resign and run the business from our home, the familiar pattern emerged once again. The demands of family, home, and children drained my profits, leaving me in a familiar state of financial depletion. This had happened to me the third time round.

In this region, when women start running their own businesses and doing well, their husbands often take a step back, believing in their capabilities to manage the financial aspects independently. This shift in responsibility distribution places a heavier burden on the women, leading to increased stress and financial strain. Unfortunately, my third business fell prey to the same fate as my first and second. It was a crushing blow, and I found myself back in the throes of depression.

Desperate for a way out, I brainstormed, searching for a solution to the recurring pattern of failure. I felt compelled to return to what I knew best: my craft business. Crafting was my sanctuary, my passion, something I never grew weary of. I can stay up all night working on my crafting projects. So, I decided to give that business idea a second try. I started the business and quickly decided to hire a small team to help me.

Contrastingly, if I were still at the bank, I'd be dozing off at my desk rather than being awake and enthusiastic about my craft. This realization keeps me doing all I can to continue doing what I love. Embarking on this journey presented several challenges, particularly at the outset. While I managed to sell off my previous ventures, the capital accumulated wasn't enough to establish the craft business I envisioned. The craft industry necessitated the acquisition of machines and tools, which were exorbitantly priced, even for used ones. Securing these tools proved to be a significant obstacle.

I initiated my craft business by obtaining a few manual tools and gradually building from there. I would acquire one or two tools at a time, feeling grateful for even those modest additions. Yet, challenges persisted, with months passing without any revenue. This dearth of funds triggered periods of deep depression, prompting self-doubt and the question of whether I'd made an irreversible mistake.

From the onset of my very first business venture, getting feedback to help me figure out solutions to the challenges I face was almost non-existent. With no siblings to lean on — I am an only child — I withdrew, erecting emotional barriers around myself. This isolation only compounded the challenge of finding solutions to my problems.

Without anyone to turn to for advice or support, I began navigating the business landscape in a trial-and-error fashion. Many attempts met with failure, and I faced a series of disappointments. However, with three failed businesses in my back pocket, I learned to strike a balance and brought that lesson into my current venture. When the orders weren't coming in, I dug into what I had previously learned and implemented different strategies, and surely enough, I started receiving more orders. My approach to Instagram shifted; I became more proactive, setting and meeting targets determinedly.

A pivotal moment arrived when I decided to disregard others' opinions entirely. It was at this point that things began to change for the better. Liberated from societal expectations, I discovered newfound determination and drive. Admittedly, societal norms had held me back. People around me had certain expectations about how my business should look and operate. The pressure to conform and meet these standards was stifling. I postponed participating in fairs, waiting for the right time to secure a high-end store complete with all the necessary machinery. I wanted to meet the societal perception of success. However, this mindset constrained my growth. It was a pivotal realization that freed me from these constraints. If I didn't take charge of my own destiny and ignore others' judgments, I'd remain stagnant indefinitely.

I came to understand that many women shared this predicament. I connected with other women facing similar challenges, and we formed small support groups. Conversations revealed that many women felt the need to match societal expectations and launch businesses in grandiose settings, like plazas or malls, rather than starting small. For me, this narrative of "fancy or nothing" held me back. Eventually, I decided to move beyond these norms. Together with my husband, we made decisions that aligned with my business aspirations. We relocated to a smaller apartment, channelling the money saved from rent into my business. This strategic move allowed me to devote more resources to my craft business.

Once settled, I explored new avenues for expansion. I began teaching crafting skills, including crochet and sewing, to children at local schools. This initiative not only boosted my business but also opened doors to contracts. I realized that I needed to prioritize my goals over others' opinions. This shift in mindset propelled my progress. Challenges persisted, and not all were easily overcome, but they became opportunities for growth. Some challenges remain vivid memories, while others have blurred over time. Nevertheless, each hurdle has played a role in shaping my journey. My craft repertoire extends beyond paper crafts; I design and craft bags, including laptop and school bags. Additionally, I specialize in upcycling, transforming discarded tyres into unique chairs. The machinery required for my diverse crafts is crucial to my business's success.

Navigating through my business journey posed distinct challenges, one of which cantered on the perception of my physical stature. When I'd approach potential clients, their gaze would often linger on me, assessing my appearance. I'm neither imposing nor diminutive in size; I fall somewhere in between. Nonetheless, scepticism would manifest in their expressions. They'd question if someone like me could manage the job, hold a drill, or bear the weight of a tool. I'd be met with statements like, "You look so delicate. Maybe we should assign a guy to do this." Despite my assurances that I was hands-on and actively involved in the work, doubts lingered. Some would even assume I had male staff taking care of the heavy lifting.

This challenge persisted for quite some time, leaving me to contemplate how to surmount it. Convincing clients that I, as a woman, could confidently handle the tasks at hand felt like a constant battle. Their scrutiny of my physicality, and by extension my abilities, was disheartening. To counter this, I began showing videos and photos of me in action, whether it was handling tools or completing various tasks. These visual aids often acted as a turning point, where some would agree to give me a chance. In certain cases, potential clients would visit me at home to see me in my workspace, eager to witness me in action firsthand. It was a significant barrier to overcome, and over time, this issue subsided as word of my capabilities spread.

Another set of challenges originated from my personal life experiences. Growing up as an only child, I developed an aversion to uncertainty and the prospect of failure. The fear of not succeeding was paralyzing, and I constantly sought to avoid situations where failure was a possibility. However, this mindset hindered my growth as it discouraged me from venturing into new territories. Gradually, I understood that failure was an essential aspect of progress. Embracing the idea that failure was a stepping stone to success allowed me to move beyond my fear.

My personal history also demonstrated the necessity of stepping out of one's comfort zone from a young age, but I had not fully understood the lesson until much later. A pivotal moment arrived when my mother arranged for me to move into a separate dwelling due to ongoing tensions at home when I was 18 years old. This move marked my departure from what I deemed my comfort zone. Initially, it was a challenging transition, but this change proved to be an essential step toward my development. It was then that I began to realize the extent of my own capabilities. This experience mirrored the progression in my business journey. Once I left the confines of what felt familiar and secure, I discovered strengths and capabilities I hadn't recognized within myself.

Through university, marriage, and other life experiences, I developed self-reliance. This personal growth, stemming from moments of independence and resilience, helped me shed my need to rely heavily on others. Over time, I embraced the idea that self-sufficiency was not only possible but essential. The lessons learned during this period were profound, teaching me that I could handle situations on my own without constantly seeking assistance.

Another significant breakthrough occurred when I realized the importance of taking action, even in the face of imperfection or uncertainty. Often, I had been held back by the belief that everything needed to be meticulously planned and flawlessly executed before I could begin. However, this mindset had paralyzed me. The turning point was understanding that progress stemmed from taking the initial step. Starting, regardless of whether things were fully in place, became a mantra for progress.

Failure, a concept I had once loathed, transformed into a valuable learning experience. The fear of it no longer had power over me. I learned that embracing failure, learning from it, and adjusting my approach were instrumental in my growth. The fear of being rejected or hearing "no" gradually dissipated, freeing me to pursue opportunities more confidently.

Ultimately, the most vital lesson was the significance of taking action, of moving forward. Regardless of my past or circumstances, the decision to move and initiate change lay with me. Looking back, I realized that regardless of the hurdles life had thrown my way, they had shaped my resilience and tenacity. Whether times were prosperous or challenging, the memory of my journey remained, serving as a potent source of motivation.

The culmination of these lessons and experiences crystallized into a powerful conviction: movement is the catalyst for progress. It became clear that waiting for the "perfect" conditions only stifles advancement. Whether it is selling beans or rice, the starting point is crucial. The size or scale doesn't matter; the act of beginning does. This awareness liberated me from the grip of stagnation, enabling me to forge ahead despite uncertainty or potential setbacks. With each stride forward, I internalized the mantra of "just move," recognizing that movement itself carried me toward a future full of potential. So, I leave you with this: Just move.

Who is she?

Loreen Aisha Ochefu-Ogiri, a mother of five from Nigeria, is a dynamic DIY craft enthusiast with a keen entrepreneurial spirit. She holds a B.Sc. in Accounting; however, she seamlessly balances motherhood and her passion for crafting in her craft business, Aiyeshaz Craft House. Loreen's artistic talents shine through her innovative creative projects, and she's inspiring others to explore their inventive side through teaching and mentorship.

Loreen's drive for entrepreneurship has led her to establish successful ventures, proving that with determination, one can turn a passion into a thriving business. Loreen embodies the spirit of a multifaceted modern woman, embracing family, education, creativity, and entrepreneurship.

"Movement is the catalyst for progress."
- **Loreen Aisha Ochefu-Ogiri**

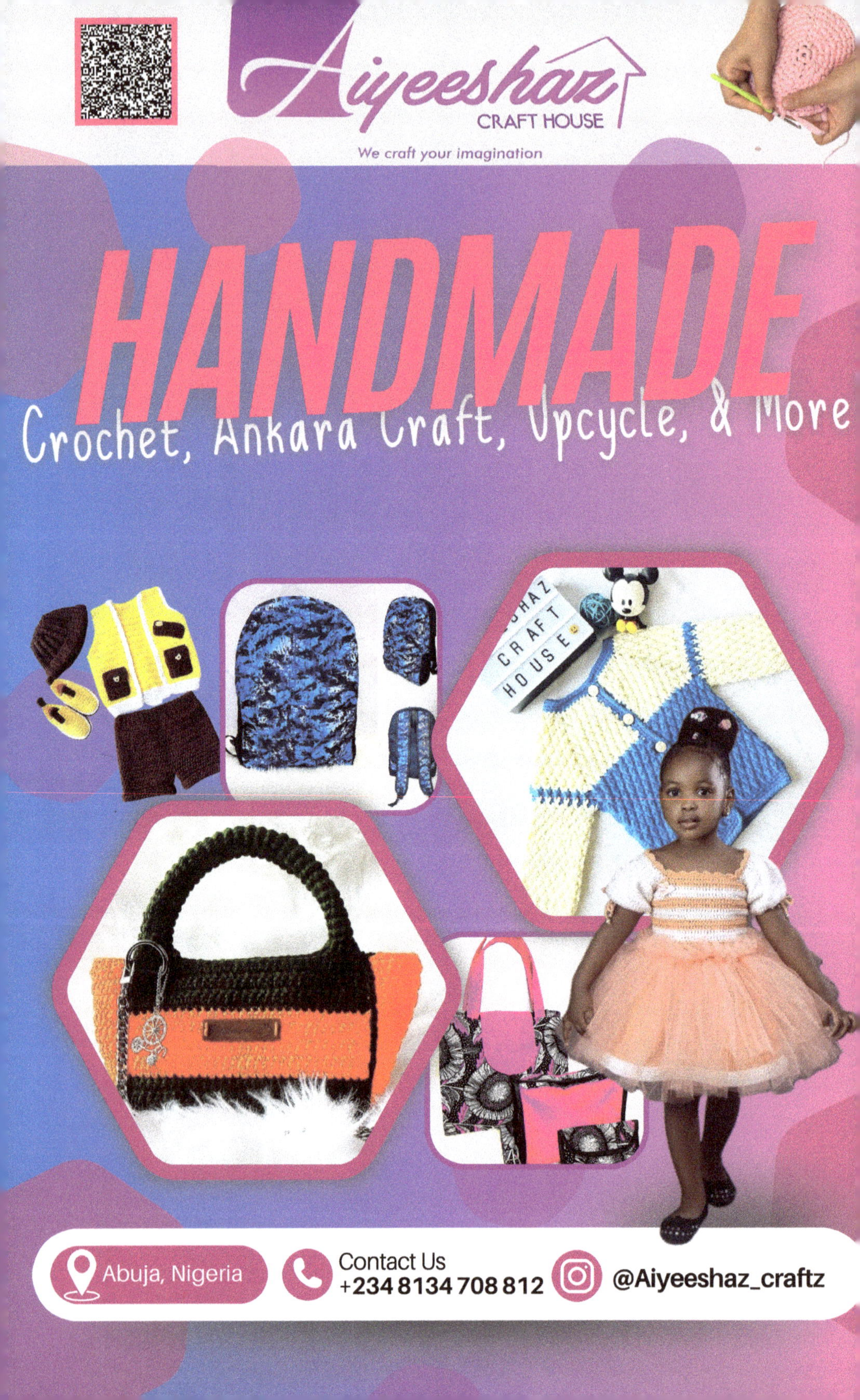

HANDMADE
Crochet, Ankara Craft, Upcycle, & More

📍 Abuja, Nigeria   📞 Contact Us +234 8134 708 812   @Aiyeeshaz_craftz

Omotinuola Oladeji

A Visionary Entrepreneur and Inspiring Philanthropist

"When faced with obstacles, it's essential to evaluate the status quo and be open to transformative changes. Stepping out of your comfort zone can lead to tremendous growth. Embrace change as an opportunity for progress, even if it involves risk and uncertainty."

The journey of a thousand miles, they say, begins with just one step. My journey into the fashion world started with me as a professional working a regular 9-to-5, pursuing growth in the corporate world. It was an extremely busy lifestyle. Even though the official working hours was from 9am to 5pm, which amounts to eight hours, I spent way more than that each day getting to and from work.

Many of my colleagues were consistently too occupied to spare time for considering their attire. However, in contrast, I was a fashion-conscious individual with a knack for sketching. Despite my busy schedule, I managed to carve out time to sketch ideas for my tailor. I was deeply invested in how I presented myself, both for work and church. I took a special interest in collaborating with my tailor, ensuring my sketches were brought to life accurately. Even when the final design diverged from my original sketch, I ensured its proper execution.

In contrast, my colleagues seemed excessively engrossed in their work responsibilities. Their attention was predominantly fixated on job performance and the advancement of their careers. Prioritizing promotions and pursuing professional development courses, they disregarded their own appearances. I, however, couldn't adopt the same approach. Despite my dedication to career growth in the corporate world, I refused to neglect my personal style.

Women working the traditional 9-to-5 were fond of appearing stylish and professional, yet their busy schedules left them with little time to visit tailors for fashionable office attire or to craft exquisite outfits for "owambe," the renowned Lagos parties. Most settled for whatever was available rather than the attire they truly desired. This was a departure from my approach, as my wardrobe was characterized by stylish and trendy ensembles. Every time they encountered my outfits, they couldn't help but remark on the distinction.

As compliments continued to pour in for my diverse wardrobe selections, I took the initiative to begin sketching not only my own styles but also those chosen by my colleagues and friends. My proficiency in this endeavour was natural and effortless, and I was always eager to engage in it. In return, my colleagues and friends were delighted to have the opportunity to wear stylish outfits akin to mine. Although this undertaking was not monetarily driven, the satisfaction it brought me was immeasurable. Witnessing the joy on the faces of my friends and colleagues upon receiving their sketches was truly heartwarming.

The sketches were like a promise of beauty that they could anticipate in their forthcoming attires. These sketches became the blueprint guiding their interactions with their tailors, as the transformation from paper to fabric required the skilled hands of a tailor. However, the course of this creative process was disrupted. The anticipation of positive feedback for my designs was met with disappointment as my friends and colleagues reported that the actual garments produced bore little resemblance to the sketches that had been conceived with such care. This deviation from my intent saddened me greatly.

Simultaneously, I had been seeking guidance through prayer due to my strong Christian faith and belief in fulfilling God's purpose for my life. I shared my disheartening experience with other tailors with my elder sister, who suggested a novel approach: why not collect fabrics from those who admired my outfits and craft the attire myself? This idea lingered in my mind.

Coincidentally, a friend from my church, employed at a multinational corporation, approached me one day. She had an upcoming significant event and insisted that I design an outfit for her. Despite my lack of confidence in executing her vision, I agreed to take on the challenge. I purchased the necessary fabric, she provided her measurements, and to my astonishment, the resulting attire was a perfect fit. Her elation was palpable, and it brought me immense joy. This success served as an epiphany, leading me to consider the possibility of transforming this passion into a viable career.

Having firmly accepted that this was the career path I wished to embark upon soon after, I initiated discussions with my tailor, who held a pivotal role within this new initiative. I articulated my intention to him, explaining that the sketches I had been crafting for my friends and colleagues were not translating into the splendid attires I had envisioned. I conveyed my desire to collaborate with him by utilizing the fabrics they provided to create the garments. Moreover, I openly disclosed my newfound aspiration to my friends and colleagues, the very individuals for whom I had been creating sketches. I made it clear that my sketching services were no longer a complimentary endeavour, but a business undertaking.

I detailed the proposition: they could entrust me with their chosen fabrics, and in turn, my tailor would expertly manufacture the attires based on my designs. This fusion of sketch and garment would ensure their satisfaction moving forward. I ensured that all relevant parties involved in this venture were duly informed and engaged. Foremost among these stakeholders were my tailor and my colleagues, with whom I discussed every facet of my journey into fashion. Even the christening of my endeavour with the name "Tsmart" was a collective decision; I shared the name with them, and they concurred that it was a fitting and commendable choice.

Finding immense joy in discussing the concept with the pertinent parties, I discovered that the mere act of sharing my vision was deeply satisfying. As I progressed to assemble my ideas into a cohesive business plan, I requested fabrics from my colleagues. With Waheed, my accomplished tailor, committed to actualizing these designs, the business commenced in earnest. Alongside this, I took steps to officially register my company's name.

In the midst of this transformation, I realized that my enthusiasm for my conventional 9-to-5 job was waning. Concurrently, the fulfilment I experienced from the process of sketching, witnessing these designs manifest as tangible creations, and delighting both my customers and myself was a daily occurrence. It was then that I understood my prayers regarding my life's direction had been answered. Rather than persisting in the confines of a traditional office job, I embraced a new routine, spending my working hours at the tailor's shop.

My company's motto, "Bridging the gap between busy women and the tailor shop," encapsulated my mission. Prior to this undertaking, there existed a disconnect: my colleagues and friends lacked direct access to my tailor, and vice versa. My time spent at the tailor's shop exposed me to various tailoring techniques, most notably the precision involved in taking measurements for clients. I acquired a range of skills, including measuring, customer pricing, operating sewing machines, mending buttons, adhering fabric reinforcements, and other fundamental tasks.

During the years I collaborated with Waheed, I absorbed a significant amount of informal training, particularly in the art of crafting garments. However, I recognized that his business model was not conducive to emulation, lacking the allure and potential for success that I envisioned for myself. It was evident that I needed to move beyond this phase and strive to fulfil my dream of establishing a prosperous career within the fashion industry.

The practical skills honed during my time at the tailor shop proved invaluable. I could expertly manipulate fabric, decipher complex styles, adeptly operate the sewing machine, and craft textiles with finesse. With conviction, I ventured forth into the world of fashion independently, departing from the shelter of Waheed's guidance. However, recognizing the gaps in my knowledge — particularly in structuring and operating a thriving enterprise — I decided to seek comprehensive education. This prompted my enrolment in fashion school, business school, and leadership school. I also secured a mentor proficient in both the fashion and business domains, who guided me in the art of managing a successful fashion house.

The bounty of knowledge accrued was immense. The completion of my course in fashion school enriched me with a broader skill set, including pattern drafting, digital sketching, and bridal wear design. Energized by my newfound proficiency, I initiated a conversation with my family regarding my aspiration to commence clothing production from our single-room apartment. With their support, I acquired manual sewing machines, enlisted the help of local tailors, and initiated the process of bringing sketches and customer designs to life within the confines of our home.

Steering the operation with meticulous attention, I managed all aspects of the business — from customer acquisition and design sketching to fabric creation, delivery logistics, and procurement of sewing materials. The business flourished within our confined space, a room that eventually metamorphosed into an exclusive workspace as my family transitioned into larger accommodations.

However, the business had outgrown our initial setting, prompting a relocation to Oworonshoki, a suburban enclave of Lagos. In this new locale, Tsmart Fashion World expanded its horizons. Equipped with electric sewing machines, I recruited a blend of professional and local tailors, and embarked on a journey to establish Tsmart Fashion World as a prominent force within the fashion industry. As the shop thrived, we even secured an additional room at the same location to accommodate our expanding enterprise, a testament to the progress and success that followed.

Tsmart experienced rapid and substantial growth, with its foundational mantra of catering to every woman's fashion needs, regardless of social class or budget, still guiding our expansion. The company had achieved a level of financial capacity that allowed for strategic planning and advancement.

During our quarterly business evaluations, we discerned that physical space played a significant role in attracting the calibre of clients required to meet our revenue objectives. We recognized that elevating our customer base could concurrently elevate our revenue. This realization prompted a comprehensive study of upscale locations within Lagos that could potentially draw the clientele we sought. After exploring various options, we eventually settled on Opebi in Ikeja, the capital of Lagos.

With a clear understanding of the positive impact this move could have on our revenue, Tsmart established a 12-month timeline for relocating from Oworonshoki, a suburban district of Lagos, to the more affluent area of Opebi in Ikeja. Notably, the funds required for this transition did not come from external sources or grants. Instead, the capital was sourced internally from the profits generated by the existing shop and workspace in Oworonshoki. We diligently allocated a significant portion of our profits towards expanding the business.

As Tsmart embarked on this ambitious journey, the aim was not only to enhance our physical location but to also amplify our market presence and ultimately secure a more robust financial standing within the fashion industry.

The transition from Oworonshoki to Opebi, Ikeja marked a significant transformation for Tsmart Fashion World across all facets of operation. This change was substantial in every sense: our rent increased by a factor of five compared to Oworonshoki. Consequently, our workforce expanded in both size and quality. This move exposed us to a broader spectrum of society, including local, national, and international clientele. We engaged influencers to promote our brand, effectively amplifying our market presence. This shift elevated Tsmart Fashion World to a pivotal role within Nigeria's fashion industry. During this period, we proudly launched our Ready-to-Wear (RTW) line, which made a resounding debut.

Recognizing an opportunity to make a positive impact in the community, Tsmart Fashion World initiated a summer school program to address the needs of secondary school girls awaiting university admission and senior secondary school students seeking purpose during long holidays. These students were enrolled tuition-free to learn fundamental tailoring skills over the course of a month. This initiative led to the establishment of Tsmart Fashion Academy, a comprehensive business and fashion school. Through this academy, we have successfully trained numerous students who have gone on to launch their own businesses and excel.

A novel initiative known as "Clothe-a-Child" emerged from a consideration for both the environment and the well-being of young children. The surplus waste generated by our factory was being discarded until I envisioned repurposing these materials to craft dresses for girls aged 2 to 10. This initiative, born out of a desire to bring smiles to children's faces and minimize waste impact, became a cornerstone of Tsmart Fashion World's Corporate Social Responsibility (CSR). The dresses are produced and then distributed to various suburbs of Lagos, bringing joy to young recipients.

Additionally, we introduced Tsmart Fashion Hub as part of our expansion efforts. This hub provides a shared space for complementary fashion items such as shoes, bags, jewellery, underwear, perfumes, hair products, and fabrics (ankara and lace). The Fashion Hub streamlines our customers' experience by offering a comprehensive shopping destination. When customers visit our establishment, they can efficiently complete their shopping for a wide range of fashion essentials without the need to travel to multiple locations.

Throughout its 18-year journey, Tsmart Fashion World has encountered a range of obstacles, each distinct to its particular phase of development. The company's evolution has been marked by varying degrees of challenges, each met with resilience. At the inception of Tsmart, the vision for the business was not as expansive as it is today.

Over time, the company has overcome numerous hurdles to reach its present status.

One of the initial challenges was the limited physical space available to run the operations. The company's growth trajectory necessitated an increase in workspace, progressing from sharing a single room apartment with my family to now occupying a dedicated three-room space solely for the factory. This expansion has been pivotal in addressing the space constraints, and Tsmart aspires to continue this momentum by aiming to acquire an entire building for its operations.

A persistent stumbling block has been the inconsistent or insufficient power supply. In the early stages, the company was heavily reliant on government-provided electricity due to financial constraints that prevented the establishment of alternative power sources. However, Tsmart has since invested in alternative power solutions, enabling a seamless transition in case of power outages.

The challenge of human resources has also been a notable obstacle. In the nascent stages, limited financial resources hindered the employment of highly skilled staff. However, as the company matured, a shift occurred, and the emphasis on employing individuals with substantial expertise and exposure became paramount.

Access to funding has been a recurring setback, with limited or no government grants or loans available. My approach to addressing this obstacle has involved turning to family and friends for support, often securing soft loans to navigate financial needs.

Despite these challenges, my perseverance, adaptability, and dedication have propelled the business forward. The company's growth trajectory and continued success demonstrate its ability to overcome barriers and thrive in the dynamic landscape of the fashion industry.

Tsmart Fashion World's journey is a quintessential grass-to-grace tale, evolving from a humble origin of sketching designs for friends and colleagues. The company's inception was rooted in my desire to translate these sketches into tangible, beautiful attires. From initially outsourcing customers' fabrics to another tailor for production, the pivotal moment arrived when I decided to break free from the confines of comfort and self-sufficiency. This courageous move marked the birth of Tsmart Fashion World as an independent entity.

This decision triggered a trajectory of unprecedented growth and advancement for Tsmart Fashion World. It ushered in an era of continuous progress, characterized by our commitment to pushing boundaries and ascending to new heights. Each subsequent decision became a strategic move aimed at propelling the company towards elevated levels of achievement.

To Black women who are pursuing their entrepreneurial dreams, I want to leave you with three pieces of advice. First, embrace courageous decisions and change. Tsmart Fashion World's success is because of my willingness to make bold decisions that deviate from my comfort zone. When faced with obstacles, it's essential to evaluate the status quo and be open to transformative changes. Stepping out of your comfort zone can lead to tremendous growth. Embrace change as an opportunity for progress, even if it involves risk and uncertainty.

Secondly, continue to learn and adapt. The success of my business underscores the value of constant learning and adaptation. Recognize that challenges are inevitable in entrepreneurship, but they also help you to grow. Seek out education and training, whether through formal institutions or mentors, to address gaps in knowledge and/or skills. Adaptability and a growth mindset are crucial for navigating the dynamic landscape of business.

Finally, leverage networks and collaborations. I have shared with you my progression from sketching for friends to establishing a prominent fashion house, and I hope that this demonstrates the power of networking and collaboration. There are many Waheeds out there who are willing to work with others to make both your dreams a reality. Find them. Surround yourself with a supportive community of peers, mentors, and partners who can provide insights, guidance, and potential collaborations. Collaborations can amplify your business's reach and capabilities, while a strong network can offer emotional support during challenging times.

Incorporating these lessons into your entrepreneurial journey can empower you to overcome struggles, ignite growth, and build a robust and successful business. Remember that challenges are opportunities in disguise, and your ability to navigate them will set the stage for lasting success.

Who is she?

Omotinuola (Tinuola) Oladeji, an exemplary businesswoman and creative force, holds the titles of Creative Director/CEO of Tsmart Fashion and Founder at Mywarehouse.ng. Her journey is a testament to relentless determination, marked by triumphs as an award-winning serial entrepreneur, investor, speaker, teacher, and philanthropist.

Tinuola's ascent to success is characterized by her unyielding spirit and a trailblazing vision. From humble beginnings, launching her Fashion venture from a modest apartment, she has emerged as the driving force behind multi-million naira enterprises. Having founded her Fashion business in 2005, she now presides over a thriving enterprise with a cutting-edge studio in Opebi, Nigeria, in an industry that brims with fierce competition.

Throughout her remarkable journey, Tinuola's faith has served as the cornerstone of her accomplishments, with her firm belief in God as the anchor of true success. A beacon of inspiration, her mission extends beyond personal achievements, aiming to illuminate the path to sustainable businesses that cultivate employee growth.

Tinuola's commitment to community betterment shines through various impactful initiatives she spearheads:

1. **Cancer Awareness Month:** Every October, Tinuola's company rallies awareness efforts and fundraising to provide free breast and cervical screenings to women in her community, championing preventive healthcare.

2. **International Women's Day Celebration:** Recognizing the immense roles women play in their households, Tinuola treats women to a day of pampering, learning, and networking. This event underlines the importance of self-care and empowerment.

3. **Clothe-a-Child Initiative:** With a heart for the underprivileged, Tinuola has clothed over 5,000 children in underserved areas like Somolu, Bariga, Ilaje, Makoko, and Ipodo, ensuring warmth and dignity for young lives.

4. **Scholarship in Fashion Designing for Girls and Women:** Through her Fashion academy, Tinuola has provided free training to over 600 women, empowering them with marketable skills and opportunities.

5. **Gratitude Dance:** To combat depression and spread positivity, Tinuola initiated the "Gratitude Dance" movement, encouraging a mindset of contentment, joy, and happiness through the hashtag #thepeoplepeoplegang on Instagram.

6. **Random Acts of Kindness:** A crusader of kindness, Tinuola leverages her platforms to inspire small acts of benevolence, fostering a culture of compassion and understanding.

Beyond her entrepreneurial pursuits, Tinuola Oladeji serves as the Principal/Lead and Instructor in Tsmart Fashion Academy and is the visionary Founder of Mind Champion. This platform imparts the wisdom of harnessing the subconscious mind's potential and elevating one's frequency for personal growth and transformation.

Tinuola's accomplishments have garnered her numerous awards. Her influence extends across media platforms, including features on Wake Up Nigeria, TVC, Punch Newspaper, and even The Living Faith Church, Canaanland.

Embracing a global perspective, Tinuola is an active member of local and international business associations. Through her diverse initiatives, she embodies the ideals of compassionate entrepreneurship, empowering individuals to create meaningful change within their communities. Her legacy is one of empowerment, resilience, and commitment to making the world a better place for all.

"Adaptability and a growth mindset are crucial for navigating the dynamic landscape of business."
- **Ọmotinuola (Tinuola) Oladeji**

5 Ojolowo Street, Off Samuel Awoniyi Street, Off Salvation Road, Opebi, Ikeja, Lagos Nigeria

+234 814 749 9813

@tsmart.official

www.tsmartfashion.ng

@tsmartfashion

DISCOUNT CODE: TSM/GIFT/Z1X23

Mrs Omitade Omoshalewa

Equitable and Inclusive Business

"It is very important for society to recognize the unique challenges we as women face, so as to work towards creating a more equitable and inclusive business environment for women, who are powerful visionaries."

One thing I've always said to myself is "Keep it going, Shalewa. One day, you will tell your story and it will inspire a lot of women." Now, here I am sharing a bit of that story in hopes of inspiring Black women in business.

The first thing that I want to draw on to inspire you is a quote from J.K. Rowling, who said, being a woman, "We do not need magic to change the world, we carry all the power we need inside already." I firmly believe this and want you to as well. As women, we have the innate power to be and do so much in the world.

Growing up as a girl child and a first girl in an African home comes with a lot of responsibilities even from a tender age. Undoubtedly, it can be overwhelming and one can build up resentment from having to take on so much at such a young age. I can admit that it was often a lot to take on. Nonetheless, all of it made me strong, balancing out my life, my activities of daily living, as well as my dreams and passion.

In terms of my background, I was born into a polygamous family in the mid-80s, grew up with my big family, went to school, and then started life proper…lol

Let me also let you know that my father passed in the early 90s, which left my mother with so much responsibilities and non-stop bills. I mean, I was only seven years old and still in primary school at the time of my father's death. I saw my mom strive so hard to pay our bills and put food on the table with no help or anything from anyone, except God. It was not easy. You know, watching her struggle so much, I remember saying to myself, "I wish my mother could have seen the future before all these things she's going through. I wish she had chosen a different life and didn't have to go through any of it." I thought it was too much for one person to have to deal with and couldn't imagine going through it myself.

I couldn't see my future and didn't know what was in store for me either, but I knew that I did not want to have such a difficult life. I promised myself, "Whatever it takes, I must work hard and smart to have a better life," if for nothing, for my mother and for my unborn children.

Thankfully, I got through secondary school successfully. It meant that I would have a chance at a better life — at the life I wanted for myself. I knew for sure that I wanted to go to university, and while waiting for Uni, I started a trade — buying and selling. I would buy pants and resell, then gradually, bras and men inner wears. I also went on to add selling nightwear to my list as the business grew.

We have a very popular and big market in the state of Lagos called Eko Market and that's where I would go to get my inventory from. Now, this is where my business journey all started. In the course of going to Eko Market, I would also run errands for people. Everyone believe they can only get the best wholesale deal in said market, so I would take their lists of all they needed and buy them at the market. While at it, trust the businesswoman in me to add a bit of extra to the items I bought for them. Some would even pay me a service charge for going on these errands. By this time, my mum had moved us back to Akure with her, so I'd have to travel quite a distance to Eko Market.

As I was running this informal business, I realised that most of my customers would ask me to buy fabrics on my errands. It was possibly the most ordered product at the time. So, I sat down and thought to myself, *Why not start a trade in fabrics? I could buy fabrics of my own and sell them on to my customers.* Well, good idea but, unfortunately, with not much savings, I couldn't afford the capital needed to invest. I wasn't going to let this deter me, though, so I came up with a grand idea that would allow me to start the business without the upfront capital. Instead of buying all the fabrics that I thought people would like, I took pictures of the different fabrics available in the market, then showed them to people around my neighbourhood. They would choose what they wanted and pay me upfront. I would reprice the fabric, adding my profits and expenses, then they would place their orders at the new price. Just like that, business got going.

I was able to run the business successfully this way for a while. Then boom, social media came along. We had BBM and then later WhatsApp, then came Instagram. I won't even lie; Instagram changed the game for my business in so many ways. It did me a lot of good and helped me evolve in my business. We should really have a talk on social media and entrepreneurship (#smiles). Now, let's focus on this discussion on entrepreneurship.

Entrepreneurship is the process of developing, organizing, and running a business to generate profit, which of course, also involves taking financial risks. Now, let's apply this to a woman. Naturally, women thrive a lot in business but are faced with certain challenges and engagement, which tend to limit or become barriers to their business activities and progress. These challenges can arise due to gender bias, social expectations, cultural stereotypes, etc.

Access to funding is one of the biggest challenges faced by female entrepreneurs. Women in entrepreneurship often struggle to secure funding for their businesses due to gender bias in the financial industry. Women-owned businesses receive only a small fraction of venture capital funding compared to male-owned businesses. So, women entrepreneurs often also face gender bias in the business world such as the assumption that they are not committed to and are not capable of running businesses.

Women entrepreneurs often have to balance the demand of running a business with demands of caring for their home and family. This can be challenging for women who have children. Most times, women also lack support networks that their male counterparts have, which can make it difficult for women to access the mentorship, networking opportunities, and also some resources they need to support and grow their businesses. Despite all of these challenges, with the right support and resources, women entrepreneurs can overcome any obstacle and build successful businesses.

It is very important for society to recognize the unique challenges we as women face, so as to work towards creating a more equitable and inclusive business environment for women, who are powerful visionaries. We should support their businesses by buying their products and/or services, even referring people to those around us, and leaving very positive reviews when we are happy with the products and/or services that we receive. This will help her financially, and also show that you believe in her vision.

As an experienced entrepreneur, you can provide mentorship to other female entrepreneurs, especially those who are new in business or those who are struggling to build their businesses. Share your insights and experiences; give advice on how she can navigate any challenge she has or that might arise. I'm sure this will be valuable support and encouragement for her. You can even introduce her to other entrepreneurs, investors, and/or potential partners, who can be of help in her growing and building her business. If you have resources to invest in her business, consider it, as it can be a significant source of support for a woman entrepreneur, which will even make her achieve her goals faster.

Please advocate for women entrepreneurs; speak up for her when you notice any form of discrimination; encourage people to recognize her achievements, and support her. It will help foster a more inclusive society and create greater opportunities for women. Remember, supporting a woman is not just good for her, it's good for everyone. This will build a more innovative and diverse economy. It will create jobs and foster entrepreneurship as a whole.

Who is she?

Mrs. Omitade Omoshalewa, a trailblazer in the field of trade, stands as a beacon of inspiration and accomplishment to those who have had the pleasure of meeting her. Based in the vibrant town of Ondo in Nigeria, she has established herself as a visionary entrepreneur and the CEO of Becca Trade Services.

Born on April 15, 1986, Mrs. Omoshalewa's journey has been one of perseverance and growth. Founded on the values of planning and personal development, she constantly seeks new avenues for progress. Her determination is palpable in every venture she undertakes, from navigating challenges to seizing innovative opportunities.

With an acute ability to identify and solve problems swiftly, Mrs. Omoshalewa showcases her commitment to detail in all aspects of her work. Her journey has been marked by achievements that mirror her adept problem-solving skills and her deep understanding of the trade landscape.

Beyond her professional accomplishments, Mrs. Omoshalewa is a woman of diverse interests. Her passion for marketing drives her to create compelling narratives that captivate audiences. Alongside her professional pursuits, she finds solace in the culinary arts, crafting flavours that tell stories of their own. When it's time to unwind, she enjoys immersing herself in the world of cinema, discovering the magic of storytelling through movies.

Mrs. Omoshalewa possesses a skill set that reflects her dedication and expertise. Her mastery of marketing, coupled with impeccable time management and communication skills, has propelled her to excel in her business. Her journey is a testament to her commitment to personal growth and her passion for entrepreneurship.

As an accomplished entrepreneur, Mrs. Omoshalewa's mission is to inspire others to follow their dreams. Through Becca Trade Services, she hopes to continue to make a lasting impact on the trade industry.

"Remember, supporting a woman is not just good for her, it's good for everyone."
- **Mrs. Omitade Omoshalewa**

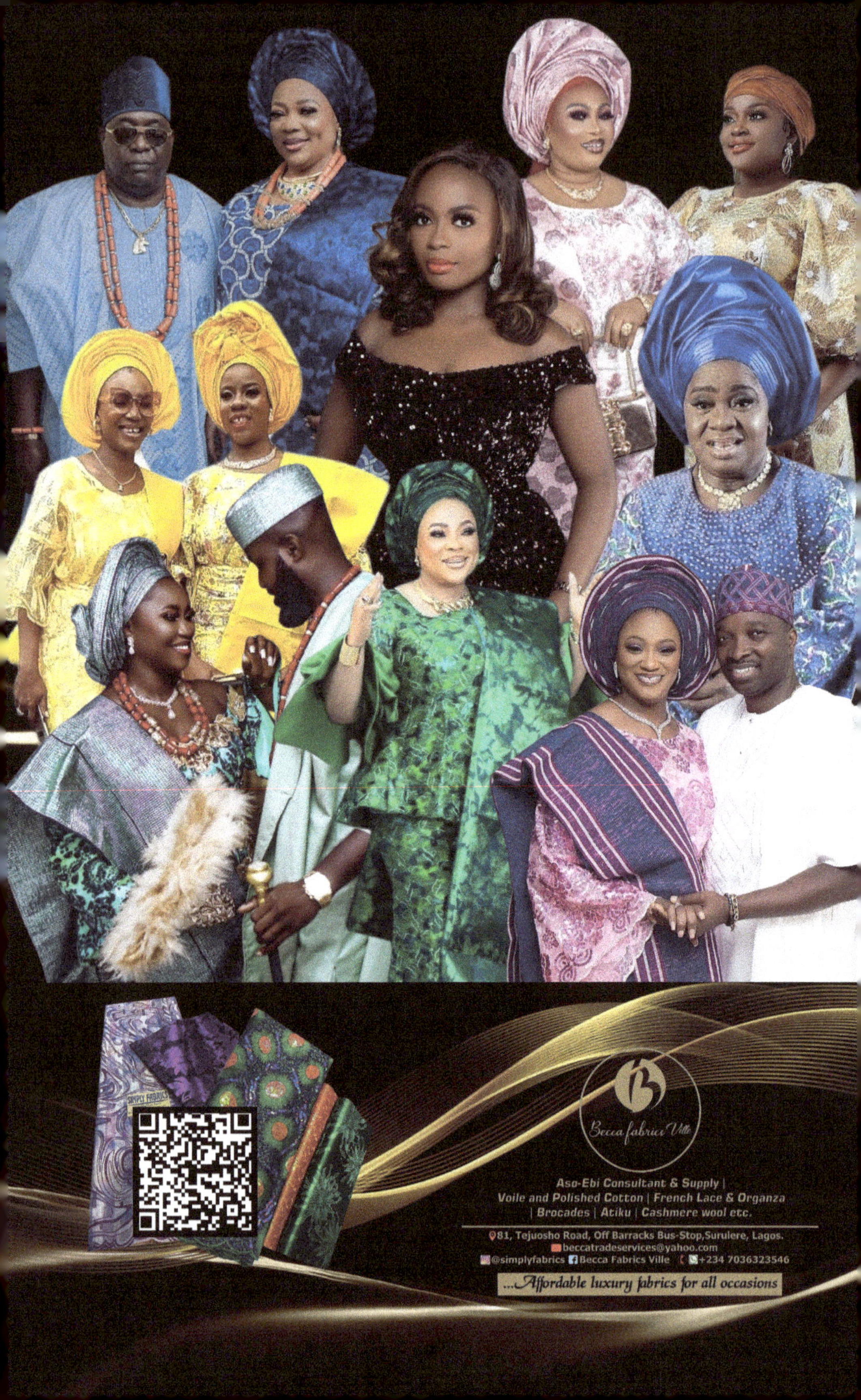

Becca fabrics Ville
Aso-Ebi Consultant & Supply |
Voile and Polished Cotton | French Lace & Organza
| Brocades | Atiku | Cashmere wool etc.
81, Tejuosho Road, Off Barracks Bus-Stop,Surulere, Lagos.
beccatradeservices@yahoo.com
@simplyfabrics Becca Fabrics Ville +234 7036323546
...Affordable luxury fabrics for all occasions

Nikki Porcher

Quitting has Never Crossed My Mind

"Keep doing the work you're doing because you're always planting seeds. Even though you don't know if or how those seeds are going to grow, or where they might take you, you're going to have full circle moments where they manifest into something real."

Years ago, I shattered my kneecap while I was sumo wrestling. It was so bad that I had to get surgery, which I was anxious about at the time. After the surgery, my doctors told me that I would probably always walk with a limp and wouldn't be able to run for long periods. This was despite the fact I was young and otherwise healthy. So, I decided that just because they were giving up on me, I wasn't going to give up on myself. I'm the type of person who's going to work as hard as I can to prove that I can do something if you tell me that it's impossible, so I was also motivated to prove them wrong!

Of course, I did physiotherapy and all the things that I was supposed to do, but I started running as a form of therapy and release as well. I trained myself until I was able to run half marathons. Then I decided I was going to run a race in all 50 states — to travel and see the world while I was at it. Subsequently, I started traveling to run half marathons and as of June 2023, I've run 21 half marathons and even the New York City Marathon, which was always a dream of mine. The fact that I ran one of the biggest marathons in the world when I was told that I'd never be able to run long distances at all is proof that we're limitless. That is precisely why we should never let anybody tell us what we're capable of. Their limiting beliefs can become our reality before we've even had the chance to figure out what we can really do. Therefore, don't let others limit you, in your personal life or as an entrepreneur. This is the first lesson.

The main reason I'm sharing this story is because I started Buy From A Black Woman after missing a flight to run a half marathon. On my way to Florida to run a half marathon, I missed my flight. I was so upset that I had to do another form of therapy — retail therapy that is. I found this shopping event online, but when I got there I discovered that I was the only Black woman there. And it's not just that I was the only Black woman who was a shopper, there were no Black women vendors either, which was outrageous because this was in Atlanta, the Black Mecca. There's no shortage of Black women business owners in Atlanta.

Anyway, there was this one woman who was selling lip balm who caught my eye. Her lip balm was $20 and she had sold out! She was just collecting people's email addresses because she had no more product. This was in 2015 before I'd started my entrepreneurship journey, so I asked her why she was collecting people's email addresses and what she was going to do with them. She told me she was going to email each person when she had more lip balm in stock so they could buy some. This was my first real introduction to consumer email marketing. I had never heard of it before or witnessed it, so a light bulb went off in my head. I wasn't on any Black women's email lists or getting emails from them about their products, but this was definitely something that Black women should and could be doing. Everything happens for a reason. This made me think that this was the reason I missed my flight.

I immediately knew that I wanted people to buy from Black women, but how? How would they know where to go, what to buy, and why they should buy from Black women? I figured I would start and share what I was buying as a form of encouragement. I could create a blog and share what I bought, and tell others where they could buy the products from as well. As a result, I created a blog and called it *Buy From A Black Woman*. I blogged about unique brands that I found, from nail polish to cotton candy, and there was even a woman who had a mail service, so I was sending letters to my friends and family using her mail service. Then I would challenge others to *Buy From A Black Woman* as a call to action.

The blog took off! People started reaching out to me, asking how they could learn about more businesses and advised me to create a directory. Black women business owners were reaching out to ask how they could be featured on the blog. They wanted to send me their products and I explained that the whole point was to buy from Black women, so I needed to purchase their products. But it wasn't until people started asking how to donate and contribute funds to what I was doing that I knew it was bigger than just a blog.

At the time, I was working in the nonprofit sector where I was always told, "You want people to spread awareness about your cause, but you also want people to donate." People were already doing both! I became intrigued. I started looking into how to start a nonprofit and began doing some research. I looked for grants for Black women who wanted to start businesses and nonprofits and there weren't any, which was another gap I discovered. The fact that there were no directories or grants just for Black women business owners made me think that this was the space I was supposed to be in; I already had experience with both. Over time, it became increasingly evident that this work was my true calling, prompting me to take a leap of faith.

I created the Black Woman Business Grant and applied for nonprofit status. This was all within the first six months of 2016. We created the grant, awarded the grant to a company called Ivy's Tea (now known as Flyest), and the same day that we were going to call our recipient, Shanae Jones, to tell her that she was receiving the grant, I received my 501(c)(3) status paperwork from the IRS. The official paperwork stating that Buy From A Black Woman was a federally registered nonprofit organization. That's when I knew that this was exactly what I was supposed to be doing with my life; which is probably why I've never had a moment where I felt like quitting.

I'm fuelled by something deeper than myself, so quitting is not an option. Having experienced the systemic issues that Black women face, I know how important it is to support Black women business owners. I've seen how supporting them transforms whole communities. I also know how much more work we need to do to achieve parity, so I have no choice but to keep pushing. I have no choice but to get creative when I encounter challenges. It's my only option. And because this work is so deeply connected to my purpose, it actually gives me energy even when I'm wrestling with challenges. So, do work that brings you closer to your purpose and allows you to harness your true energy, and you will never fail. That's the second lesson.

Having a higher purpose attached to your work also makes it easier to see obstacles as puzzles that just need solving, which makes it easier to attempt to do impossible things. It's less daunting because you're just focused on doing the best that you can, even when you aren't exactly sure where you're going or what the outcome is going to be. It's during this process that you learn how to keep doing the work, despite the absence of immediate results, which is something that you have to master as an entrepreneur anyway.

There are so many seeds that you're going to plant, and the growth of the trees they become may remain unseen until they're ready to sprout. Sometimes, you won't ever see them, but in the interim, practice listening to what your purpose calls for. As you go through this journey, you may have to overcome obstacles, get over the fear of rejection, remove your ego so you can let go of the need to control the process, and keep reminding yourself that you're on the path of bigger and better things. I promise you; you'll start to see signs and receive affirmations from the Universe. Confirmation that you're exactly where you're supposed to be. A good example of this is back when I was invited to speak at the *Move Something! Conference* alongside incredible speakers like Tabitha Brown.

The first time I heard about the *Move Something! Conference* in 2015, it was from a DJ I was dating because he was commissioned to do the music for the event. As I heard him working on this playlist, there was one song in particular that I was completely obsessed with, *Dionne* by Osunlade. It led me to find *Walk The Way You Talk* by Dionne Warwick and the lyrics have become a living mantra for me:

> *"Just because you said things have got to change*
> *They won't go away*
> *Nothing goes away*
> *Not unless you do the things you promised to*
> *So walk the way you talk and talk the way you walk*
> *Saying something's wrong isn't good enough*
> *That won't make it right*
> *Gotta make it right*
> *And the only way is doing what you say*
> *So walk the way you talk and talk the way you walk…"*

I believe in the power of speaking what you want in order to manifest your goals, wishes and desires, but you have to do the work! So, the song resonated with me, and the conference did too. The more I learned about the conference, the more I thought that I'd like to speak at the event. This was before I had a platform, a blog, or even an idea about what I would actually talk about. I knew this was something I wanted and something I was going to do even before Buy From A Black Woman was established.

Fast forward to 2019, I was invited to speak at this same event. When the promos for it came out, this song that I was obsessed with way back in 2015 was what they used for my promo! They don't know my backstory (I don't even know if I was dating who I dated!), so they had no idea of my connection to the song and the synchronicity of it all, which just goes to show how amazing the Universe is. I also got to see Ms. Dionne perform this song in 2022 in Vegas and I cried like a baby, but that's a different story for a different day. I have so many moments like this that I can't even explain because of how crazy they seem. Sometimes it feels like my life is a movie, but this is just how the Creator shows you that you are on the right path and doing the things that you're supposed to be doing with your life.

I've always asked for signs. I ask for signs to guide me through my life and help me navigate challenges, so this wasn't anything new. But it's always an amazing time when I receive them and this one set the tone for what was a very memorable event. However, it is important to note that if I hadn't done the groundwork to build Buy From A Black Woman into what it is, I never would have gotten to share my words, gifts, and knowledge with such an amazing community of like-minded women. Keep doing the work you're doing because you're always planting seeds. Even though you don't know if or how those seeds are going to grow, or where they might take you, you're going to have full circle moments where they manifest into something real. This is the third lesson.

When you look back and see the value of all that work you put in, the experience you gained along the way, and the skills you developed solving those supposedly impossible puzzles, it will all make sense. Of course, this doesn't mean that the challenges will end. The more you do, the more they will come. I'm almost 10 years into this journey and still overcoming challenges. The more you overcome, the easier they become. It might help if you think of challenges as pop-quizzes to remind you of the lessons you've learned.

Who is she?

Nikki Porcher sees challenges as unsolved puzzles, making the journey of overcoming obstacles an outlet for her creativity rather than a mere struggle. This distinctive mindset has been her guiding force, propelling her to thrive in various demanding environments such as the underfunded public school system, the armed forces, and understaffed nonprofit organizations.

She is an advocate for Black women and the founder of Buy From a Black Woman. Nikki has a myriad of accomplishments, but the only one that matters to her is her efforts to keep going.

She is passionate about community development and creating a more equitable future for Black women. Her commitment to this cause flows effortlessly as she pours her heart and soul into everything she does. Nikki welcomes collaborations and partnerships that align with her mission for lasting change.

"There's a lesson in everything."
- **Nikki Porcher**

848 Oglethorpe Ave. SW #10873
Atlanta, GA 30310

www.buyfromablackwoman.org

info@buyfromablackwoman.org

Making *the room* bigger for *Black* Women to move in.

We support Black Women.

Educate
We work hard to provide the best tools and resources to help start, build and sustain Black Women Business Owners. This includes our workshops, webinars & video content.

Empower
Our Black Woman Business Grant is our flagship financial empowerment program helping black Women Business Owner take their ideas to next level.

Inspire
Inspire others to support and buy from Black Woman. Grab your official Buy from a Black Woman merchandise in our Inspire Store.

Partnerships & Features

THEA   H&M

The New York Times   MBE

SWAY   HUFFPOST

Living proof.

Bloomberg   WWD

The Hollywood Reporter

ALJAZEERA

Patrice Reid

Transforming the World of Skincare

"Success is not solely measured by monetary gains. The path may be challenging, but remember that success often lies on the other side of perseverance."

Serendipity! The trajectory of my life changed. In 2018, my eczema was at its worst, aggravated by the ineffective products I was using. The topical steroids my doctor prescribed weren't working; actually, they made my condition worse! It was then that I decided to go back to my roots and start making my own skincare products.

Being a lover of natural herbs and science, and a biochemistry student from the Northern Caribbean University, I had always enjoyed experimenting with different formulas and concoctions. So, I delved into extensive research, attended courses, and spent countless hours perfecting my product formulations. Little did I know that this seemingly small endeavour would soon become my life's passion.

As I began using my handmade skincare products, my eczema started to improve, and people around me started noticing the transformation. They would ask me about the products I was using, and on occasion, I would share my creations with them. The positive feedback was overwhelming, and the demand for my products began to grow.

What started as a hobby quickly evolved into a full-fledged business. In 2019, I found myself unable to continue giving away free products due to the mounting costs. However, customers were more than willing to pay for the exceptional results they were seeing on their skin.

With the support and encouragement of those around me, I took the leap and turned my passion into a business. The journey was exhilarating, and some days, I found myself running out of products and having to take preorders. The dream of Fervour Amour skincare was finally taking shape.

However, as fate would have it, just as my business was gaining momentum, the world was hit by the unforeseen COVID-19 pandemic in early 2020. I was placed on unpaid leave from the airline company I worked for, as flights to Jamaica were suspended. It was a devastating blow, and I found myself at a crossroads: Should I pack up my dreams and move back home, or should I invest all my savings in my business during such uncertain times?

It was a decision that weighed heavily on my mind. The logical choice seemed to be to give up on my dreams and seek stability elsewhere. Established businesses were crumbling around me, and the world was shrouded in uncertainty. But deep down, I knew that giving up was not an option. I couldn't ignore the burning passion inside me, urging me to take a chance on myself.

I made the seemingly impossible decision. I would put all my savings into my business and face the challenges head-on. I needed to adapt quickly to the changing circumstances and find ways to keep my business afloat.

I started by creating a professional website, revamping my labels and packaging, and expanding my product line. The pandemic had forced me to think outside the box and find innovative ways to reach my customers. I worked tirelessly, as if my life depended on it, because in many ways, it did.

The road ahead was not easy. Financial constraints and self-doubt threatened to derail my entrepreneurial dreams. But I refused to let adversity define me. With the support of my family, friends, and incredible customers, I pushed through the challenges, one day at a time.

In the middle of these struggles, I had a stroke of luck; I met Sheldon Harris through a mutual friend. He saw the potential in my business and offered guidance during the Fervour Amour rebranding exercise. His advice was invaluable, and I will forever be grateful for his mentorship. I also decided to take a course in entrepreneurship, which helped tremendously.

Through all the trials and tribulations, I learned some valuable lessons that I believe every aspiring female entrepreneur should embrace. Firstly, never give up on your dreams, especially when they seem impossible. It is during these moments of doubt and uncertainty that our truest potential emerges. Stay determined and persevere, even when the odds are stacked against you.

Secondly, surround yourself with a support system that believes in you. Entrepreneurship can be a lonely journey, but having a network of family, friends, and mentors who uplift and encourage you can make all the difference. Their belief in your capabilities can fuel your determination and keep you going, especially when self-doubt creeps in.

Lastly, stay humble and prioritize your happiness throughout the entrepreneurial journey. It's easy to get caught up in the chase for success, but it's essential to remember the joy and passion that brought you to this path in the first place. Success is not solely measured by monetary gains. The path may be challenging, but remember that success often lies on the other side of perseverance. Keep pushing forward, and let your entrepreneurial dreams soar.

Who is she?

Patrice Reid, a dynamic entrepreneur and skincare enthusiast, has made a significant mark in the business world with her passion for creating effective and natural skincare solutions. With a background in biochemistry from the Northern Caribbean University and a certificate in small business management from The University of West Indies (UWI), Patrice's dedication to her craft is evident through her numerous accomplishments and ventures.

During her time as a student, Patrice demonstrated remarkable resilience and determination by working three jobs alongside her studies. As a student recruiter, hotel receptionist, and teacher's assistant at the Northern Caribbean University, she developed excellent time management and multitasking skills. She also gained valuable experience in the aviation industry, working for Ajas Aviation Services on contracts with United Airlines and Swoop Airlines.

However, it is in the entrepreneurial space where Patrice truly thrives. Starting her journey with companies like Avon, Amway, and Cool Buzi, she honed her skills and learned the ins and outs of the business world. In 2015, she founded her first company, Rapido Spices, which garnered significant attention for its innovative seasoning tenderizer. Patrice's hard work and determination paid off as she won three business competitions, including the title of Most Innovative and Best Business Plan for 2016.

Today, Patrice's focus lies with her latest venture, Fervour Amour, a natural skincare company dedicated to providing solutions for individuals with skin conditions such as eczema and sensitive skin. With global shipping capabilities and plans to expand into stores in Vietnam by 2023, Fervour Amour is set to become a formidable force in the industry.

Beyond her impressive entrepreneurial achievements, Patrice is passionate about giving back to her community, particularly the younger generations. She frequently engages in small talks at schools, facilitates school tours, and shares her knowledge of entrepreneurship with students. In addition, she actively donates to various charities and participates in fundraising events and health fairs.

When she's not busy running her business or giving back to her community, Patrice indulges in her love for traveling, particularly enjoying water sports and nature. Her fondness for animals, especially dogs, is a testament to her compassionate nature. With a knack for cooking inherited from her chef parents, Patrice loves experimenting in the kitchen and seeks out new culinary experiences in restaurants, both locally and internationally.

Patrice's mission is to provide safe and effective skincare solutions to individuals worldwide, promoting body positivity and self-confidence. She is committed to being a trusted source for those transitioning from topical steroids or chemical-filled products to more natural alternatives that allow their skin to thrive.

Originally from St. Mary, Jamaica, Patrice now calls Montego Bay home. As a proud member of the Branson Centre of Entrepreneurship Caribbean community and a member of the Jamaica Business Development Corporation, she continues to make her mark and inspire others in her quest to empower individuals and transform the world of skincare.

"It is during these moments of doubt and uncertainty that our truest potential emerges."
- **Patrice Reid**

Dikeledi Ndoni Sibanda

When Passion and Creativity Meets Entrepreneurship

"As an entrepreneur, there are many self-taught mechanisms to help you navigate making profits and remain relevant with your product, seek them out and make use of them."

My name is Dikeledi Ndoni Sibanda: A South African queer activist/human rights defender, who has worked in the activism/human rights sector for almost 18 years. I started out as an admin, outreach officer, and project coordinator, and have been doing activism through media advocacy work for the last few years. Born and bred in the township known for riots in the early 1990s, Katlehong in Ekurhuleni, east of Johannesburg, I hold qualifications in media practice (film/television), public relations, and photography. Thus, I am also a visual artist and entrepreneur. I also played soccer for a lesbian's team — Chosen Few — that was doing activism through sport. We have travelled worldwide, participating in the Gay Games, including in London at the UK Federal Gay Games. I love traveling to other countries to learn different cultures while enjoying myself at the same time.

I am passionate about creativity and interlinking my work, hobbies, and the things that I love doing. Hence, I had the idea of making "rainbow clothing" whilst still working at the Forum for Empowerment (FEW). This Black lesbian organization works to promote and defend the rights of Black queer women in South Africa. In all honesty, I never took it seriously at the time; more so because I hardly had time to do anything outside of work. My job entailed supporting women and documenting cases of hate crimes and GBV. However, when I was promoted to project officer for the Soweto Pride March, I decided to express my creativity regarding our marketing and advertising materials. I designed a rainbow t-shirt with an African Map written, "Soweto Pride March." This t-shirt became one of our visibility tools. Queer people wanted to buy them; bear in mind, this was during the early 2000s when rainbow clothing was not as popular as it is now.

As I was growing in my activism and media advocacy journey, I then realized that I love money and I needed to balance my activism work and my personal life/needs. By this time, I was working in a call centre, and in a job that I did not enjoy at all. The thing is that life experiences will sometimes make you learn and be humble as well as present you with things that don't even resonate with your values or are not passionate about. However, that job played a massive role in my business today. In that position, I learned so much about customer service (soft and hard skills alike), and I now appreciate that experience.

I have also ventured into the production media business where I worked with visual artists. We started a production company to document workshops, conferences, and events for organizations and companies. It was through this experience that I truly understood the meaning of "everything happens for a reason." While working at the call centre in 2019, my business partner approached me and said, "I know you are over your work, and we want to start our business. I want us to buy ice cream machines and start that business." She added, "I have done research on it and the pricing of the machine, but to start this business, it is way expensive." We then had to think of other options to make money to buy these machines. I told her that I wanted to do a rainbow clothing and winter jackets line since we were approaching winter, which would allow us to generate the money we needed to get the ice cream machine. I produced a couple of jackets, and people showed interest; however, we were met with a few challenges — I had challenges with couriers as well as sizes and had to put a hold on the jackets. It was not doable at the time. I learned that I needed to set up things correctly.

When the COVID-19 pandemic hit in 2020, our business really started. My partner and I were both working from home, so we had plenty of time to think about things. With so much silence around those days, one could think about anything and everything. It could make anyone go crazy but it gave us the space we needed to think about business and where we wanted to be.

I bought a pair of stylish plain red tracksuits during the lockdown. I loved them and suggested to my business partner that we purchase and sell some of these tracksuits while we were still thinking of another plan. She thought they were excellent — comfortable, warm, and stylish — tracksuits that people could wear as most of the country was working from home. With the two of us being photographers, I wore the tracksuit I had purchased and we did photoshoots. We discussed the name of our business and came up with the name Colour Central; this would allow us to do so much without limiting ourselves. We wouldn't have to stick to selling these tracksuits forever. It would give us the opportunity to develop and grow our business.

We did an excellent shoot with that red tracksuit and put up a perfect marketing strategy with just one tracksuit. We posted photos on our social media and made it clear that they came in different colours. We delivered around Johannesburg; remember, at that time, it was a challenge to go out to do your shopping due to restrictions. We had a permit to move around, which was an advantage. People showed interest in our tracksuits and wanted to see the other colours they were available in. Without a budget, we were determined to not let it get in the way of the business taking off. My partner and I went to the shop where I'd bought the tracksuits and asked to take pictures in them. I explained that I wanted to sell them and the seller was okay with that. Hence, they became our suppliers.

In essence, we started our business with just my red tracksuit and an ordering process that we agreed on with the supplier. We would put in a deposit and pay the rest on delivery. Once an item sold, we would have to deduct the deposit, balance, and delivery fees. Then we were left with our profit. We started our business with nothing. We made a lot of money with this strategy and wanted to grow the business from there. We got to understand the market better and found out where to get more products to sell to our market. We learned to buy in bulk and benefit from discounts.

This then gave us the opportunity to re-introduce rainbow clothing, and that side of our business started picking up more than we expected. Remember, we didn't spend anything on starting our company; well, except for my red tracksuit, but we were able to grow it. With this side of the business coming to life, though, we started facing many challenges. People now wanted customized products that we couldn't find. Rainbow material was and still is an issue to find, unless you improvise, do sublimation, or digitize it, which could be more pleasant for our creative standards. I found a woman who was a seamstress and suggested to my business partner that I we checked with her to see if she could help us with bringing the designs that were being demanded to life. She said it was doable and gave us some advice, and boom, we could meet our customer's needs through designs and sewing their garments from scratch. This was still during covid. We have since expanded our business post-covid, selling at markets, events, and even in our homes.

Currently, we have rebranded. Printing, branding, and textile are what we excel in, and our focus is more on that. We continue doing activism through clothing (rainbow clothes). Our goal is to have physical stores across the country as well as find ways to take our brand to the global market. We are doing what we love and the feedback we get means everything to us. What is so strange is that most of our rainbow clothing customers are heterosexuals and young teenagers who are queer and want to express themselves and be visible by wearing our merchandise. One nonbinary teenager at our stall said, "This bracelet is a confirmation of my being and how I would like to express myself to my parents, family, and society." This struck our attention as we've had so many good and affirming comments from both parents and kids.

We have some success stories before we can mention our other challenges. In late 2020, we applied for a small grant for printing equipment with Gauteng Enterprise Propeller (GEP). We got a response in 2021 where we received an appointment to get essential printing equipment to enable us to design and print for ourselves. This has allowed us to make a reasonable profit as it has removed the need to add a relevant third party to our business revenues. Through our collaboration with a well-known queer activist, Bev Palesa Detsie, a South African lesbian artist and filmmaker, we were able to raise funds for her medical fees. We made and sold branded merchandise with the picture illustration of her face, such as t-shirts, hoodies, sweaters, and tracksuits. This was our first prominent branding gig and collaboration, which put us on the map and strengthened our reach even abroad. Through this partnership, we designed branding and printing textile for well-known production companies and organizations such as Redemption, Seriti, Burnt Onions, Iranti-org, Multi-Pek, and Global Network of People Living with HIV, and "Its' Feminist thing," a TV show.

Collaboration/partnership work can be a big gain for most small businesses. It can help SMEs reach a broader market, which our business has proven thus far. Choosing to sell our products through different avenues such as markets, for example, has also changed how we generate revenue. In most cases, we would be the only ones selling rainbow clothing at different venues, which is an advantage.

Starting a business is more challenging than it sounds; there are many challenges pre, during, and post building a company. For example, although our collaboration with Bev was a success, we faced challenges with getting products to customers abroad because of the costs associated with shipping. It has been difficult sustaining our target market as our rainbow clothing is not in demand all year round; most of our sales are during Pride months. The added challenge is that there is more competition in the market now and most people know where and how to access our competitors.

Funding to secure office space and other resources is a considerable challenge when you don't know where to go or who to contact. We have people duplicating our merchandise to the point where we hear of people being scammed by people misusing our marketing materials. They contact us for refunds on items that are not bought from us. This is a hard place to be in as a business but what it has taught us is that our marketing strategy is still one of our challenges. We need to be consistent and put in place a strategic plan that will work for us for the long term. A plan that will make it less likely for anyone to defraud consumers pretending to be us.

We have faced many other challenges in our business, big and small, and you will too. However, you need to keep up and maintain your brand through various platforms and networking. Business needs attention and maintenance like any other relationship that involves people and money. As a business, we aim to remain creative and find ways to set us apart as we continue to produce special and stylish inventory. We want to evolve to the point where we open opportunities for young unemployed youth in the design, branding, and creative field.

As an entrepreneur, there are many self-taught mechanisms to help you navigate making profits and remain relevant with your product, seek them out and make use of them.

Who is she?

Dikeledi Ndoni Sibanda is a South African queer activist and human rights defender with a remarkable journey spanning nearly two decades. Born and raised in the vibrant township of Katlehong, Dikeledi's life has been a fusion of passion, activism, creativity, and entrepreneurship.

At the start of her activism and human rights work, Dikeledi's initial roles included administrative work, outreach coordination, and project management. However, it was her fervour for media advocacy that defined her recent years in the field. With a background in media practice, public relations, and photography, she seamlessly wove her artistic inclinations into her activism.

Dikeledi's activism extends to sports, specifically soccer, taking her all over the world. She is presently partner and founder at Colour Central. This company, initially inspired by a pair of red tracksuits, has designed branding and printing textile for well-known production companies and organizations including Redemption, Iranti-org, Multi-Pek, and Global Network of People Living with HIV.

"Business needs attention and maintenance like any other relationship that involves people and money."
- **Dikeledi Ndoni Sibanda**

COMPANY BRANDING

FULLY CUSTOMIZABLE

featured in
media.

feel the special
handcrafted goodness.

Premium corporate and business apparel

made from scratch by our dedicated team of seamstresses.

We only produce products of
quality and satisfaction.

Colour Central

CONTACT US
+27 83 360 6082 / +27 81 774 6371
info@colourcentral.co.za
www.colourcentral.co.za

PARTNER WITH US

From a professional standpoint, branded products largely serves as a lasting impression long after you've left the meeting with your potential investors, partners, or clients. Our range of corporate gifting solutions includes branded notebooks, diaries, coffee mugs, pens, laptop bags, you name it, we have it! Whether individually or in small groups, Colour Central has the best solution for you.

Collaborations

We partner with artists and thought leaders to advance worthwhile causes.

EVENT BRANDING

We carefully source and brand conference packs and other supplies for your specially invited guests, including itineraries.

SCAN

We look forward to working with you;
thank you.

Veneish Tanneisha Wallace

Quality Caregiving is Underpinned by the Innate Human Spirit

"Allow your resilience to be an evolving force — a firm belief that within you lies the power to transform hardships into stepping stones, to chart new paths, and to emerge from the darkness stronger, wiser, and more determined than ever."

From the very outset of my journey, hurdles seemed to appear at every turn. Reflecting on those formative years, the memory that stands out the most was when I decided to take a firm step towards realizing my aspirations as an entrepreneur. I was determined to break the cycle and embark on the path of business ownership, but little did I know the complexities that would follow.

It all began with a conversation I had with my mother, a person whose unconditional love for me was undeniable. She had always stood by me, supporting me as a mother should, and she held onto her visions for my life. However, her vision for me was shaped by a world that might not have fully recognized the less-travelled path I was about to tread. I can't fault her for that; after all, she only knew the life she had lived. The generational patterns cast a shadow on her understanding of the possibilities that lay before me. The weight of conformity and the comfort of familiarity coloured her perspective.

I made the decision to start my business and shared my intentions with my mother. I expected encouragement — a shared excitement to embark on this business endeavour. To my surprise, her response was laced with scepticism. "That'll work," she said, her sarcasm cutting through my enthusiasm like a sudden gust of wind extinguishing a flickering flame. Her reaction struck me with a mixture of confusion and disbelief. This was my plan, my dream, and I had believed that her unconditional support would naturally follow.

In that moment, we sat across from each other, the minutes ticking away in a silence that seemed to stretch endlessly. It was a pivotal crossroads, a moment where my will power was tested in the face of scepticism. I found myself questioning my concept, the business I had envisioned. I could feel the seed of uncertainty taking root within me.

With her seemingly simple words, my mother unintentionally ignited a storm of introspection, but I knew I couldn't give up on the idea because I felt it deep within my core. I knew this was the right path for me. That night, I was so hurt that I didn't even stay at my mother's, though that was the original plan. I wanted to be alone — to dig deep and find the courage to move forward. At home and alone, in those moments of contemplation, I realized that the key to my decision-making was nestled within myself. It wasn't just about seeking external approval or validation; it was about aligning my choices with what resonated deep within me. I discovered that the feeling of rightness resided in my chest, an intuition that spoke louder than any external noise.

With that newfound clarity, I recommitted to my entrepreneurial aspirations. I harnessed the strength within me to start my business, to breathe life into the concept that had stirred my soul. I was met with challenges and faced uncertainties, but I forged ahead, determined to turn my vision into a reality.

My mother's belief in my capability grew with time, even if it took her a while to fully grasp the scope of my dreams. The journey towards becoming the strong woman I am today, a successful businesswoman, was marked by the struggles to overcome generational patterns and the courage to step into unfamiliar terrains. It taught me the importance of trusting my instincts and staying true to my dreams, even in the face of scepticism from those who usually believe in and support us.

The journey I embarked upon as an entrepreneur was riddled with obstacles that forced me to confront my limits, recalibrate my perceptions, and reevaluate my strategies. One significant challenge that emerged was the task of sourcing and placing women caregivers within home healthcare. The intricacies of this venture were not immediately apparent; they unveiled themselves through a series of interactions that highlighted the complexities inherent in this field.

Home healthcare is a domain that demands not only skill and expertise but also a profound understanding of the human element that underpins caregiving. My initial aspiration was to facilitate a synergy between skilled caregivers and those in need of their services. Yet, the reality I encountered was a blend of personal expectations, financial constraints, and unforeseen dynamics.

As I delved into the process of recruitment and placement, I discovered a poignant truth: not all caregivers are alike. The disparity between aspiration and reality became evident when I realized that not every caregiver shared my dedication, my struggles, and my financial limitations. It's a stark realization that we often face differing circumstances, perspectives, and motivations. While I was striving to make ends meet and carve out a space for myself as an entrepreneur, I encountered caregivers who had their own aspirations, often diverging from the path I was navigating.

For some, the financial element loomed large in their motivations. They entered this field with an eye on monetary gain, sometimes at odds with the holistic approach I envisioned. The challenges I faced mirrored my own struggles as they negotiated a world that demanded compromises between personal and professional aspirations. A recurrent theme emerged — managing the delicate balance between financial considerations and the quality of care provided. This balance was a delicate tightrope that I sought to tread, ensuring the caregivers understood the ethos I aimed to uphold. The tension between these two dimensions threatened to derail my business before it was even fully off the ground.

These challenges also posed an internal struggle. I was determined to provide the highest level of service while navigating the intricate web of caregivers' expectations. I had to grapple with the reality that their motives and perspectives might not align with the values that drove me. It was a lesson in understanding that the entrepreneurial journey can be hindered by individual aspirations.

What compounded this challenge was the personal investment I had in my business. Every success and every setback felt like a reflection of me. The experiences of caregivers often affected my perception of the business as a whole, reminding me of the interconnectedness of our journeys. It wasn't just about matching caregivers with care recipients; it was about bridging the gap between diverse motives and forging a path that served both the individuals in need and the caregivers themselves.

It took time, but eventually, I learned that every setback was an opportunity for growth. Every encounter with a caregiver who didn't align with my vision became a chance to refine my understanding of the industry and my own business. The learning curve was steep, and it forced me to cultivate a discerning eye — one that could identify the individuals whose motivations aligned with the core values I held dear.

This chapter of my entrepreneurial journey also paralleled my personal life, an intersection of challenges and opportunities. The complexities of home healthcare mirrored the complexities of my relationships, particularly the turning point I encountered in my journey as a woman. The lessons from one sphere resonated in the other, and I realized that the pursuit of entrepreneurship is one that encompasses personal growth, professional evolution, and the art of learning from every experience.

In retrospect, these challenges have been transformative. They have moulded me into a more resilient entrepreneur and a more discerning individual. The lessons I learned from navigating the dynamics of caregiver placement were a microcosm of the broader lessons life imparts. Entrepreneurship, like life, is not a linear path; it's mixed with challenges, discoveries, and personal growth.

Life's journey has an uncanny way of intertwining with the path of entrepreneurship, each experience leaving a permanent mark on our personal and professional growth. A pivotal moment in my journey emerged through a challenging relationship — a relationship that shook the very foundations of my identity and tested the limits of my inner strength.

When I encountered this person, I believed I had a solid understanding of who I was and where I was headed. I carried within me the truth of my own being, grounded in the experiences that had shaped me thus far. Yet, this relationship presented a different narrative — one that aimed to undermine my sense of self and redefine me in ways that didn't align with my inner convictions.

The impact was profound. It felt like the fabric of my being was torn asunder, leaving me shattered and struggling to reconcile the person I knew myself to be with the person I was being told I was. Words can be powerful, and the words that were spoken during this time had the potential to unravel my very identity. The accusations of inadequacy, financial struggles, and a myriad of demeaning labels clouded my self-perception.

However, adversity often has a way of birthing strength. What emerged from this crucible was not defeat, but rather a spirit that refused to be broken. I found within me a core of resilience that I hadn't fully recognized before — a determination to rise above the barrage of negativity and emerge with my self-worth intact. The fragility of my emotional state compelled me to seek refuge within myself, to silence the external voices and embark on a journey of self-discovery.

Meditation became my refuge, a space where the noise around me could be muted, and I could confront my own thoughts and fears. In the quiet moments of the morning, when the world was still and my mind was open, I delved into my spirituality with a renewed vehemence.

These moments of introspection allowed me to navigate my doubts and insecurities, uncovering the strength that laid dormant within me.

I realized that boundaries were essential, both in personal relationships and in business. The relationship I had endured illuminated the importance of maintaining my own sense of self, irrespective of external opinions or expectations. This realization extended to my entrepreneurial journey. Just as I needed boundaries in my personal life to protect my identity, I needed them in my business to uphold its ethos and vision.

Placing caregivers in home healthcare roles proved to be an intricate dance between understanding their motivations and maintaining the standards I had set for my business. This experience mirrored the process of setting boundaries in my personal life. I came to understand that not every opportunity, not every individual, aligned with my values. Just as I had to discern between what was beneficial and what was detrimental to my well-being, I had to make choices in my business that protected its integrity.

This wasn't the only challenge that I had to face in my business. Clientele ebbed and flowed, a reminder of the impermanent nature of success. Yet, within this ebb and flow, I discovered my unyielding resolve to adapt and persist. Every downturn was an opportunity to learn, to refine my approach, and to evolve. Just as I had learned to find my centre in personal turmoil, I found my footing even when the tides of business seemed uncertain.

A pivotal relationship, marked by challenges and transformation, illuminated the power of authenticity. When confronted by accusations that attempted to redefine my identity, I stood at the crossroads of self-doubt and self-discovery. In the wake of this storm, I emerged with a clarity that authenticity is my most precious asset. The tempest had stripped away pretences, revealing the strength in embracing my truth without compromise.

The connection between authenticity and my business journey soon became apparent. As I navigated the business home healthcare, I realized that authenticity extended beyond my personal identity. It became the cornerstone of my business ethos. My journey in caring for families transcended mere professionalism; it was about building trust and fostering genuine connections. The families I served, like the relationships in my personal life, deserved an authentic experience — one stemming from integrity and transparency.

Amidst the challenges of business, another lesson resonated profoundly: the power of perseverance. Just as relationships evolve, so do businesses — experiencing seasons of abundance and scarcity. Through these fluctuations, I learned to persist and innovate. The experience of caring for the elderly, from one generation to another, revealed a deeper understanding of the cyclical nature of life.

The intricacies of relationships also extended to the mentoring and shaping the next generation. The lessons I learned from my experiences shaped my approach to raising my daughter. I was determined to foster her independence, instil values of self-worth, and encourage her to speak her truth. This parenting philosophy flowed into my business endeavours. Just as I championed my daughter's voice, I recognized the importance of empowering my clients, understanding their needs, and advocating for their well-being.

Authenticity's ripple effect extended to friendships as well. I understood that authentic connections are marked by growth and mutual support. As my personal and professional paths diverged from certain friendships, I realized that evolving relationships were not failures, but reflections of the dynamic nature of life. Letting go became an act of self-preservation — a recognition that loyalty to my truth was paramount.

Life's journey is riddled with obstacles that test our mettle, challenge our spirits, and lead us down unfamiliar paths. Through my own personal tribulations and business hurdles, I've come to recognize that resilience isn't just an attribute — it's a state of mind, a source of strength that empowers us to surmount even the most daunting challenges.

As a Black woman navigating the complexities of life, I've embraced the truth that understanding oneself is paramount. This understanding becomes the compass that steers me through the rough seas of existence. There were moments when darkness loomed large, and I questioned my worth, my choices, my place in this world, but I knew that losing myself would be the greatest loss of all. In these moments, I discovered that within the depths of despair, a light always emerged; a whisper that said, "You're not alone. You're stronger than you know."

Amidst the trials and tribulations, my business journey intertwined with my personal struggle, creating a symphony of challenges that were meant to overwhelm me. The external façade belied the turmoil within, but through it all, I persevered. I dismantled toxic relationships that threatened to consume me, recognizing that my well-being was non-negotiable. The painful act of ending these relationships was, in fact, an act of self-preservation — a testament to my commitment to upholding my authenticity and worth.

A significant chapter of this journey involved the battle for the well-being of my child. A contentious relationship became a courtroom battle, a test of my strength as a mother and a businesswoman. Through this difficult process, I navigated the storm, emerging not only victorious but also fortified in my understanding of the power within me. This victory wasn't just legal, it was also emotional, symbolic, and a reminder that my strength, faith, and belief in myself can weather even the fiercest storms.

In times of despair, I leaned on my business with a deep sense of hope. It was a sanctuary where I found solace, purpose, and the drive to keep moving forward. Nevertheless, the weight of managing both personal and professional challenges cast overwhelming shadows. My mantra became "What can I change?" It echoed in my mind, urging me to evaluate, adapt, and thrive. Education became my tool — a means to propel my business to the heights I envisioned. Despite setbacks, I embraced the opportunity to learn, to equip myself with the skills needed to transform my vision into reality.

The most profound realization in my journey was understanding that resilience isn't born solely from external circumstances. It germinates within, cultivated by the choices we make, the perspectives we adopt, and the strength of our spirit. It's the force that carries us through moments of self-doubt.

With each trial, my resilience transformed into resilience not just for me, but for those around me — those who sought inspiration in my journey. As I weathered the storms, I demonstrated the power of resilience to my daughter, nurturing her independence, teaching her the importance of self-worth, and encouraging her to speak her truth. My commitment to authenticity and resilience is a legacy and will be an inheritance of strength passed down through generations.

Now, as I close out this contribution, I want to remind you as a business woman that challenges are a constant. It's our response to these challenges that defines us. Embrace the unknown, dance with discomfort, and view adversity as a facilitator of growth. Allow your resilience to be an evolving force — a firm belief that within you lies the power to transform hardships into stepping stones, to chart new paths, and to emerge from the darkness stronger, wiser, and more determined than ever.

Who is she?

Veneish Tanneisha Wallace, born on October 30, 1982, arrived in this world as the sun broke through the clouds, announcing her presence with a radiant touch. Her journey began in a small community named Wilmington, also known as Pilot, nestled within the heart of St. Thomas. From the very start, it was evident that the world was in need of her unique spirit.

Growing up, she navigated the terrain of her family's dynamics, shaping her into the remarkable individual she is today. Her childhood was marked by an underlying solitude, being an only child. However, this solitude paved the way for her to forge bonds with fellow children she affectionately dubbed as cousins, creating her own vibrant circle of companionship amidst the quietude.

Her educational journey commenced in Morant Bay, St. Thomas, under the care of a dedicated teacher who owned Stanton Basic School. Echoes of "bits of paper lying on the ground" resonated in the air after each school day. A brief interlude at Morant Bay All Age School was followed by a return to Wilmington Primary and subsequently, Duckenfield Primary. These formative years were marked by her resilience, strength of character, and an innate desire for solitude.

The transition to St. Thomas Technical High School marked a turning point. Here, the passion for higher education ignited within her. Amid financial constraints, she dreamed of college. The path was uncertain, but a steadfast boyfriend recognized her potential and guided her towards a brighter future. A pivotal moment came when nursing school beckoned. Doncaster School of Practical Nursing became the arena where she honed her strength and determination, crafting the foundation of the formidable business woman she is today.

Her experiences extended beyond Jamaican borders, but a deep-seated yearning for more began to stir within her heart and she wanted to build her business in Jamaica to serve her people. This yearning gave birth to Eliza Care, a company bearing the name of her grandmother, Eliza Grant. The compassionate spirit that had been passed down through generations drove her to create a venture that resonated with her roots. Eliza, her grandmother, had instilled in her the essence of caring for others. Memories of walking through Wilmington, carrying bags of provisions for those in need, etched the importance of compassion deeply in her heart.

Life's journey took her through diverse chapters, including the challenges of motherhood, the loss of a child, and moments of dancing to the rhythm of her own heart. Through it all, her faith remained steadfast. Prayer became her solace, a refuge where she sought strength even in her moments of weakness.

As a single woman in a world where so many women remain in relationships that does not elevate them, she chooses to stand firmly, refusing to settle for less than she deserves. Veneish Wallace believes that her greatness is within reach and will continue to work towards achieving it.

"Adversity often has a way of birthing strength."
- **Veneish Tanneisha Wallace**

ELIZA CARE
Kingston, Jamaica

AFFORDABLE
HOME HEALTH CARE

Eliza Care is Kingston-based business providing Practical and RN nurses for Home Health Care throughout Kingston and St Andrew.

Our Services:

- Elderly Care
- Pre/Post Surgical Procedures
- Day/Night Health Care Hours
- Cleaning of Ulcers and Wounds
- Doctor Visits
- Baby Sitting
- Medication Administration
- Dietary Assistance

Contact Us 📞 +1-876-866-0734   ✉ elizacare100@gmail.com

"You don't make progress by standing on the sidelines, whimpering and complaining. You make progress by implementing ideas."

- **Shirley Chisholm**

Closing Remarks

Through the stories shared by the women in this book, I hope you have come to realise that there is no such thing as perfection in business, or in life. As women in business, no matter how successful our businesses become, we continue to face challenges. While some are easy to overcome, others threaten to ruin the very essence of who we are. Our ability to face these challenges, finding solutions, allow us to grow personally and professionally. It helps us to build new skills that we can employ in our business relations as well as personal lives.

In sharing the stories in this book, I wanted women to understand that no matter how challenging things get, they can chase their entrepreneurial dreams. Find ways to make it happen, and more than anything, remember that you are not alone. Seek out support, look to others who have solved the problem you are dealing with, and see what you can learn from those experiences. Great businesses aren't built on the foundations of perfection but rather on the ability of those who own them to continue to find solutions for the problems that arise.

If you have a passion for business, do not take it to your grave. Your ideas can leave marks on the world and change lives in ways you can't even begin to imagine.

I hope that you will take a second look at those businesses you emulate and remind yourself that as successful as they are, they are probably overcoming difficulties every minute of the day. My hope then is that this inspires you to take on the challenge of starting your business, amidst the lack, fears, and everything else that is holding you back.

As you've journeyed through this book, you've delved into the inspiring stories of Black female entrepreneurs who have faced and conquered formidable challenges. You've seen for yourself that it is doable because others are doing it. Now, as we conclude this journey together, let me leave you with some parting words of motivation and encouragement:

Remember Your Power: You are stronger and far more resilient than you may sometimes believe. The challenges you face are not insurmountable barriers, but rather chances to help you grow and learn. Face them, learn from them, and let them empower you to persevere.

Embrace Your Unique Identity: Your identity as a Black female entrepreneur is a tremendous asset. You are indeed the biggest dream your ancestors could have conceived. Your identity can bring fresh perspectives, unique insights, and a wealth of untapped potential to the business world, so don't keep it locked away inside of you. Never underestimate the power of your individuality; it is what will set you apart.

Community and Mentorship: You don't have to walk this path alone. Seek out mentors and a support network to guide you. There are many who are willing to give back; all you have to do is find them. Use the exercises provided in the workbook as tools to help you build those crucial connections, refine your skills, and chart your course forward.

Set Goals and Stay Persistent: Sometimes your dreams will seem daunting and unachievable. However, I have always been of the belief that if the mind can conceive it, it is indeed doable. So, don't shy away. Instead, break down what seems impossible into clear, achievable goals and manageable steps. Persevere through the ups and downs of entrepreneurship, knowing that each setback is a stepping stone to your ultimate success.

Believe in Your Vision: Your dreams are valid, your vision is powerful, and your business can create positive change in the world. Believe in yourself and the impact you can make.

Stay Adaptable: The business landscape is ever-changing. Be willing to change with it to keep growing in your business. Be ready to adapt and innovate.

Keep Learning: Learning doesn't end when we graduate school. Learning is probably one of the most constant aspects of life. Never stop learning. Seek knowledge. There is always someone who knows what you want to know or a course, book, blog, etc., out there with the information you need. Go and find it. Hone your skills and stay informed about industry trends; you will do your business a disservice otherwise.

Celebrate Every Victory: From the smallest triumphs to the grandest achievements, take time to celebrate your successes. When you acknowledge your progress, it reminds you of who you are, your purpose, and fuels your passion for what lies ahead.

You Are the Future: Pursuing your entrepreneurial dreams not only shapes your own destiny but also paves the way for future generations of Black female entrepreneurs. Be the inspiration that you want to see in the business world. Be the role model that you probably never had.

Quality Over Quantity: Over time, aim to have a team of quality individuals rather than simply filling roles with people who may not be committed or reliable. Having a dedicated and capable team can make a significant difference in the success of your business.

Business is Not a Hobby: Remind yourself and your team that your business is not a hobby or a side project that you are doing simply because you want to; it's a serious venture that requires dedication and professionalism from everyone involved. Everyone must play their role to ensure the success of the business. Clearly communicate your expectations to your staff, including your commitment to maintaining high standards and the importance of respecting your business.

Now, as you embark on your entrepreneurial path, remember that every challenge you face is a testament to your strength and potential. Go on to complete the exercises provided in the companion workbook, *Great Entrepreneur in Training*, so you have some of the tools to overcome some of the hurdles you are bound to face. Stay motivated, stay persistent, and never give up on your dreams. Your business-mindedness is a force that can transform the world.

The world is waiting for your brilliance. Go out there and show the world what you are made of!

"I work really hard, but I don't feel like I'm working. It's not work when it's something you love."
- **Taraji P. Henson**

www.ingramcontent.com/pod-product-compliance
Lightning Source LLC
Chambersburg PA
CBHW041316110526
44591CB00021B/2806